Academic Encounters

2nd Edition

Yoneko Kanaoka

Series Editor: Bernard Seal

CAMBRIDGE
UNIVERSITY PRESS

CAMBRIDGE UNIVERSITY PRESS
Cambridge, New York, Melbourne, Madrid, Cape Town,
Singapore, São Paulo, Delhi, Mexico City

Cambridge University Press
32 Avenue of the Americas, New York, NY 10013-2473, USA

www.cambridge.org
Information on this title: www.cambridge.org/9781107644922

First published 1999
Second edition 2013

Printed in the United States of America

A catalog record for this publication is available from the British Library.

ISBN 978-1-107-67463-9 Student's Book with DVD
ISBN 978-1-107-64492-2 Teacher's Manual

Additional resources for this publication at www.cambridge.org/academicencounters

Layout services: NETS, Bloomfield, CT

Table of Contents

Scope and Sequence

Unit 1: Planet Earth • 1

	Content	L Listening Skills	S Speaking Skills
Chapter 1 **The Physical Earth** page 3	**Interview 1** A Geologist Talks **Interview 2** Earth's Natural Beauty **Lecture** A Look Inside Planet Earth	Listening to directions Listening for main ideas in an interview Listening for details Listening for main ideas in a lecture	Sharing your knowledge Sharing your opinion Discussing what you have learned
Chapter 2 **The Dynamic Earth** page 18	**Interview 1** Living Near an Active Volcano **Interview 2** Living with Earthquakes **Lecture** Volcanoes	Listening to numerical information about distances and rates Understanding multiple-choice questions Drawing inferences	Interpreting a map Responding to a speaker Retelling what you have heard Sharing ideas

Unit 2: Water on Earth • 41

	Content	L Listening Skills	S Speaking Skills
Chapter 3 **Earth's Water Supply** page 43	**Interview 1** Water in the United States **Interview 2** Water in Cambodia **Interview 3** Water in Africa **Lecture** Source and Functions of Surface Water	Listening for opinions Listening for details Listening for specific information	Examining graphic material Examining a map Applying what you have learned Predicting the content Considering related information
Chapter 4 **Earth's Oceans** page 62	**Interview 1** Adventure Under the Ocean **Interview 2** Surf's Up **Lecture** One World Ocean	Expressing likes and dislikes Predicting the content Listening for main ideas Thinking critically about the topic Personalizing the topic Listening for signal words	Sharing your opinion Retelling what you have heard Thinking creatively about the topic Building background knowledge on the topic

V Vocabulary Skills	**N** Note Taking Skills	Learning Outcomes
Reading and thinking about the topic Understanding word parts Examining vocabulary in context Guessing vocabulary from context	Organizing your notes in an outline Listening for supporting details Clarifying your notes with a partner Using your notes to label an illustration	Prepare and deliver an oral presentation about a natural disaster
Reading and thinking about the topic Building background knowledge on the topic Guessing vocabulary from context Predicting the content	Focusing on the introduction Using telegraphic language Using your notes to make a study sheet	

V Vocabulary Skills	**N** Note Taking Skills	Learning Outcomes
Reading and thinking about the topic Building background vocabulary Guessing vocabulary from context	Using symbols and abbreviations Using bullets and brackets to organize your notes Rewriting your notes after a lecture	Prepare and deliver an oral presentation about daily water usage
Reading and thinking about the topic Guessing vocabulary from context	Using handouts to help you take notes Focusing on the conclusion Making test questions from your notes	

Unit 3: The Air Around Us • 83

	Content	L Listening Skills	S Speaking Skills
Chapter 5 **Earth's Atmosphere** page 85	**Interview 1** Pollutants in the Air **Interview 2** Air Quality **Interview 3** Humid and Dry Air **Lecture** What Is In the Air Out There?	Listening for background noise Listening for specific information Answering multiple-choice questions	Examining a map Sharing your experience Conducting an experiment Predicting the content Applying what you have learned
Chapter 6 **Weather and Climate** page 102	**Interview 1** A Future Meteorologist **Interview 2** Severe Weather **Lecture** Global Warming	Listening for specific information Predicting the content Listening for opinions Listening for numerical information Listening for cause and effect	Personalizing the topic Understanding humor about the topic Thinking critically about the topic Applying what you have learned

Unit 4: Life on Earth • 123

	Content	L Listening Skills	S Speaking Skills
Chapter 7 **Plants and Animals** page 125	**Interview 1** A Green Thumb **Interview 2** The Galapagos Islands **Lecture** What Is a Living Thing?	Listening for specific information Listening for examples Listening for expressions of contrast	Personalizing the topic Building background knowledge on the topic Examining graphic material Thinking critically about the topic Conducting an interview Applying what you have learned
Chapter 8 **Humans** page 142	**Interview 1** Running Track **Interview 2** Eat to Live, Don't Live to Eat **Lecture** Systems of the Human Body	Listening to directions Listening for main ideas Listening for specific information Listening for expressions of time order	Personalizing the topic Building background knowledge on the topic Conducting a survey Considering related information Sharing your opinion

V Vocabulary Skills	**N** Note Taking Skills	Learning Outcomes
Reading and thinking about the topic Building background knowledge and vocabulary Examining vocabulary in context Identifying key vocabulary in the lecture Guessing vocabulary from context	Organizing your notes in an outline Organizing your notes in a chart	Prepare and deliver an oral presentation about global warming with a partner
Reading and thinking about the topic Understanding scientific symbols Examining vocabulary in context Building background knowledge on the topic Guessing vocabulary from context	Copying a lecturer's illustrations	

V Vocabulary Skills	**N** Note Taking Skills	Learning Outcomes
Reading and thinking about the topic Examining vocabulary in context Previewing the topic Guessing vocabulary from context	Checking your notes Organizing your notes in a chart	Prepare and deliver an oral presentation about a living thing in Earth's biosphere
Reading and thinking about the topic Examining vocabulary in context Building background knowledge on the topic Guessing vocabulary from context	Taking notes in a flowchart Evaluating your own note taking	

Introduction

The *Academic Encounters* Series

Academic Encounters is a sustained content-based series for English language learners preparing to study college-level subject matter in English. The goal of the series is to expose students to the types of texts and tasks that they will encounter in their academic course work and provide them with the skills to be successful when that encounter occurs.

At each level in the series, there are two thematically paired books. One is an academic reading and writing skills book, in which students encounter readings that are based on authentic academic texts. In this book, students are given the skills to understand texts and respond to them in writing. The reading and writing book is paired with an academic listening and speaking skills book, in which students encounter discussion and lecture material specially prepared by experts in their field. In this book, students learn how to take notes from a lecture, participate in discussions, and prepare short presentations.

The books at each level may be used as stand-alone reading and writing books or listening and speaking books. Or they may be used together to create a complete four-skills course. This is made possible because the content of each book at each level is very closely related. Each unit and chapter, for example, has the same title and deals with similar content, so that teachers can easily focus on different skills, but the same content, as they toggle from one book to the other. Additionally, if the books are taught together, when students are presented with the culminating unit writing or speaking assignment, they will have a rich and varied supply of reading and lecture material to draw on.

A sustained content-based approach

The *Academic Encounters* series adopts a sustained content-based approach, which means that at each level in the series students study subject matter from one or two related academic content areas. There are two major advantages gained by students who study with materials that adopt this approach.

- Because all the subject matter in each book is related to a particular academic discipline, concepts and language tend to recur. This has a major facilitating effect. As students progress through the course, what at first seemed challenging feels more and more accessible. Students thus gain confidence and begin to feel that academic study in English is not as overwhelming a task as they might at first have thought.

- The second major advantage in studying in a sustained content-based approach is that students actually gain some in-depth knowledge of a particular subject area. In other content-based series, in which units go from one academic discipline to another, students' knowledge of any one subject area is inevitably superficial. However, after studying a level of *Academic Encounters* students may feel that they have sufficiently good grounding in the subject area that they may decide to move on to study the academic subject area in a mainstream class, perhaps fulfilling one of their general education requirements.

The four levels in the series

The *Academic Encounters* series consists of four pairs of books designed for four levels of student proficiency. Each pair of books focuses on one or more related academic subject areas commonly taught in college-level courses.

- *Academic Encounters* 1: The Natural World
  Level 1 in the series focuses on earth science and biology. The books are designed for students at the low-intermediate level.

- *Academic Encounters* 2: American Studies
  Level 2 in the series focuses on American history, politics, government, and culture. The books are designed for students at the intermediate level.
- *Academic Encounters* 3: Life in Society
  Level 3 in the series focuses on sociological topics. The books are designed for students at the high-intermediate level.
- *Academic Encounters* 4: Human Behavior
  Level 4 in the series focuses on psychology and human communication. The books are designed for students at the low-advanced to advanced level.

New in the Second Edition

The second edition of the *Academic Encounters* series retains the major hallmark of the series: the sustained content approach with closely related pairs of books at each level. However, lessons learned over the years in which *Academic Encounters* has been on the market have been heeded in the publication of this brand new edition. As a result, the second edition marks many notable improvements that will make the series even more attractive to the teacher who wants to fully prepare his or her students to undertake academic studies in English.

New in the series

Four units, eight chapters per level. The number of units and chapters in each level has been reduced from five units / ten chapters in the first edition to four units / eight chapters in the second edition. This reduction in source material will enable instructors to more easily cover the material in each book.

Increased scaffolding. While the amount of reading and listening material that students have to engage with has been reduced, there has been an increase in the number of tasks that help students access the source material, including a greater number of tasks that focus on the linguistic features of the source material.

Academic Vocabulary. In both the reading and writing and the listening and speaking books, there are tasks that now draw students' attention to the academic vocabulary that is embedded in the readings and lectures, including a focus on the Academic Word list (AWL). All the AWL words encountered during the readings and lectures are also listed in an appendix at the back of each book.

Full color new design. A number of features have been added to the design, not only to make the series more attractive, but more importantly to make the material easier to navigate. Each task is coded so that teachers and students can see at a glance what skill is being developed. In addition, the end-of-unit writing skill and speaking skill sections are set off in colored pages that make them easy to find.

New in the reading and writing books

More writing skill development. In the first edition of *Academic Encounters*, the reading and writing books focused primarily on reading skills. In the second edition, the two skills are much more evenly weighted, making these books truly reading and writing books.

End-of-chapter and unit writing assignments. At the end of each chapter and unit, students are taught about aspects of academic writing and given writing assignments. Step-by step scaffolding is provided in these sections to ensure that students draw on the content, skills, and language they studied in the unit; and can successfully complete the assignments.

New and updated readings. Because many of the readings in the series are drawn from actual discipline-specific academic textbooks, recent editions of those textbooks have been used to update and replace readings.

New in the listening and speaking books

More speaking skill development. In the first edition of *Academic Encounters*, the listening and speaking books focused primarily on listening skills. In the second edition, the two skills in each of the books are more evenly weighted.

End-of-unit assignments. Each unit concludes with a review of the academic vocabulary introduced in the unit, a topic review designed to elicit the new vocabulary, and an oral presentation related to the unit topics, which includes step-by-step guidelines in researching, preparing, and giving different types of oral presentations.

New and updated lectures and interviews. Because the material presented in the interviews and lectures often deals with current issues, some material has been updated or replaced to keep it interesting and relevant for today's students.

Video of the lectures. In addition to audio CDs that contain all the listening material in the listening and speaking books, the series now contains video material showing the lectures being delivered. These lectures are on DVD and are packaged in the back of the Student Books.

The *Academic Encounters* Listening and Speaking Books

Skills

The *Academic Encounters* listening and speaking books have two main goals. The first is to help students develop the listening and note taking skills needed to succeed in academic lecture settings. The second goal is to help students build confidence in their speaking ability – in casual conversation, classroom discussion, and formal oral presentations.

To this end, tasks in the *Academic Encounters* listening and speaking books are color-coded and labeled as L 🄻 Listening Skill tasks, V 🅅 Vocabulary Skill tasks, S 🅂 Speaking Skill tasks, and N 🄽 Note Taking Skill tasks. At the beginning of each unit, all the skills taught in the unit are listed in a chart for easy reference.

- **Listening Skills 🄻.** The listening skill tasks are designed to promote success in a variety of listening contexts, from brief instructions to extended academic lectures, and for a wide range of purposes including listening for specific details, identifying general ideas, and evaluating extra-linguistic features such as tone of voice.

- **Vocabulary Skills 🅅.** Vocabulary learning is an essential part of improving one's ability to understand spoken language, especially in an academic setting. It is also key to oral expression. Pre-listening vocabulary tasks throughout the book provide context for interviews and lectures. Exercises stress the importance of guessing from context. Oral activities also include suggested words and expressions. Each end-of-unit review features both a written and oral academic vocabulary review activity to reinforce the academic words that have been introduced.

- **Speaking Skills 🅂.** The speaking skills exercises in the book are designed to introduce and facilitate the practice of language and communication skills that students will need to feel comfortable in casual social contexts as well as academic settings. They range from presenting personal opinions to conducting an interview. Language models are provided.

- **Note Taking Skills 🄽.** Lecture note taking is key to academic success, and is thus a major focus of the *Academic Encounters* listening and speaking books. In each chapter, the lecture section introduces a specific aspect of note taking, providing a focus for listening to the lecture itself and for follow-up comprehension checks. Additional non-academic note taking skills are practiced throughout each chapter and frequently "recycled" for maximum practice.

The audio program

Authentic listening material, based on real interviews and lectures, forms the basis of the chapter material. Each chapter includes a warm-up listening exercise to introduce the topic, informal interviews that explore different aspects of the topic, and a two-part academic lecture on related material. These different types of listening expose students to varied styles of discourse, and they all recycle the chapter's concepts and vocabulary.

The complete audio program is available on audio CDs. In addition, a DVD containing the lecture delivered by a lecturer in front of a classroom is included in the back of the *Student Book*. Transcripts of the lectures are also provided in the back of the *Student Book* and the complete transcript of all this listening material is included in this *Teacher's Manual*.

Tasks

Whenever a task type occurs for the first time in the book, it is introduced in a colored commentary box that explains what skill is being practiced and why it is important. At the back of the book, there is an alphabetized index of all the skills covered in the tasks.

Order of units

The units do not have to be taught in the order in which they appear, although this is generally recommended since tasks increase in complexity, and because note taking tasks may draw on skills originally presented in an earlier chapter. However, teachers who wish to use the material in a different order may consult the scope and sequence in the front of the *Student Book* or the Skills Index at the back of the *Student Book* to see the information that has been presented in earlier units.

Course length

Each chapter in the *Academic Encounters* listening and speaking books represents approximately 10 hours of classroom material. The new end-of-unit activities may take an additional 3 hours of class time. Multiple opportunities exist to lengthen the course by the addition of related material, longer oral presentations, movies, debates, and guest speakers on the chapter topics. However, the course may also be made shorter. Teachers might choose not to do every task in the book and to assign some tasks as homework, rather than do them in class.

Quizzes

The *Academic Encounters* series adopts a sustained content-based approach in which students experience what it is like to study an academic discipline in an English-medium instruction environment. In such classes, students are held accountable for learning the content of the course by the administering of tests.

In the *Academic Encounters* series, we also believe that students should go back and study the content of the book and prepare for a test. This review of the material in the books simulates the college learning experience, and makes students review the language and content that they have studied.

At the back of this *Teacher's Manual* are eight reproducible lecture quizzes containing true-false and multiple-choice questions. Students should complete these quizzes after they listen to the lecture and do all related exercises.

General Teaching Guidelines

In this section, we give some very general instructions for teaching the following elements that occur in each unit of the *Academic Encounters* listening and speaking books:

- The unit opener, which contains a preview of the unit content, skills, and learning outcomes
- The *Getting Started* sections, which help students prepare for the chapter topic
- The *Real-Life Voices*, which are short interviews with people of all ages and backgrounds on the chapter topic the chapter topic
- The *In Your Own Voice* sections, which provide students with an opportunity to discuss their own opinions on the topic
- The *Lectures*, which are at the end of each chapter
- The *Unit Review* activities, which include vocabulary reviews and an oral presentation. These are included at the end of each unit

Unit Opener

The opening page of the unit contains the title of the unit, a photograph related to the content of the unit, and a brief paragraph that summarizes the unit. Have the students discuss what the title means. Have them look at the art on the page, describe it, and talk about how it might relate to the title. Read the paragraph summarizing the unit contents as a class, making sure that students understand the vocabulary and key concepts. At this point it is not necessary to introduce the unit topics in any depth.

The second page lists the unit contents: the titles of the two chapters within the unit and the titles of the interviews and lecture in each of the two chapters. Have students read the titles and check for understanding.

After reviewing the contents, have students focus on the listening, speaking, vocabulary, and note taking skills that they will be practicing in the unit. Ask students if they recognize any of the skills listed. It is not necessary for them to understand all of the terms used at this point, since the skills will be introduced and explained when they appear in the unit. Finally, go over the *Learning Outcomes*. Explain to students that the subject matter and the language skills that they will be learning throughout the unit will help them prepare for this final oral presentation.

The unit opener section should take less than an hour of class time.

Getting Started

This section contains material that is designed to activate students' prior knowledge about the topic, provide them with general concepts or vocabulary, and stimulate their interest. The section begins with a photograph, cartoon, or image. Have students look at the image and read the questions about it. Here and throughout, maximize opportunities for students to develop oral fluency and confidence by having them answer and discuss in pairs or small groups before reviewing as a class.

A short reading related to the chapter topic follows. Have students read and then respond orally to the comprehension and discussion questions that follow. The questions are designed to go beyond the reading and elicit language and concepts that will be presented in the chapter, so encourage students to volunteer their own information and ideas.

An introductory listening activity concludes this section. The type of listening task is determined by the chapter content. It may involve completing a chart, doing a matching exercise, or listening for specific information. The task provides skill-building practice and also gives students listening warm-up on the chapter topic. Make sure that students understand what is expected of them before they listen, and replay as needed so that all students feel successful. The follow-up comprehension and discussion questions can be answered as a class, in pairs, or in small groups.

The *Getting Started* section should take about one hour of class time.

Real-Life Voices

Real-Life Voices, which contains one or more informal interviews on topics related to the chapter content, is divided into three sub-sections:

Before the Interview(s)

This sub-section contains a pre-listening task that calls on students either to predict the content of the interview or to share what they already know about the topic from their personal or cultural experience. Be sure to take enough time with this task for all students to contribute. Students can also benefit here from each other's background knowledge.

Interview(s)

Because unfamiliar vocabulary is a great stumbling block to comprehension, each listening activity is preceded by a glossed list of terms (many of them colloquial) that will be heard in the interview. Have students review the vocabulary.

The next task prepares students to understand the content of the interview excerpt that they will hear; a variety of task types are used, including true-false statements, incomplete summaries, and short-answer questions. Have students review this task carefully as it will help them focus on the pertinent information as they listen to the interview excerpt.

After they have listened to all of the interview(s) and checked their comprehension, an additional listening exercise directs the students' attention to a specific aspect of language use featured in the interview(s), such as verb tense or tone of voice.

After the interview(s)

This sub-section provides students with activities to demonstrate and deepen their understanding of the concepts presented in the interviews. It may involve synthesizing information from a short reading or drawing inferences about material in the interviews. Encourage all students to contribute their opinions.

The *Real-Life Voices* section should take three to four hours of class time.

In Your Own Voice

This section builds on the content presented up to this point in the chapter and also focuses on one or more language functions (for example, asking for opinions, expressing interest, expressing polite negatives) that either were used in the *Real-Life Voices* interviews or are relevant to discussion of the chapter topics. Semi-structured speaking activities elicit the functional language, relate to the chapter content, and encourage students to share their own information. Language examples are given. Allow students to practice the language with a number of partners, and perform for the class if they like. The focus is on developing confidence with the functional language required for casual conversation and discussion.

The *In Your Own Voice* section should take approximately one hour of class time.

Academic Listening and Note Taking

This section, which is constructed around a recording of an authentic academic lecture, is divided into three sub-sections:

Before the Lecture

This sub-section begins with a brief introduction of the lecture topic and the person who is giving the lecture. Read it as a class and ask students about any language that is unfamiliar. Encourage students to guess at the meaning of unfamiliar words.

The following task either provides background information on the lecture or elicits what students may already know about the lecture topic. Topics in the book are chosen to be of general interest, so encourage that interest in students by asking them to volunteer what they already know. Some students will likely have studied the lecture material in their first language; let them become the experts in providing context for their classmates.

Finally, this sub-section introduces a specific academic note taking skill that is determined by the language of the lecture itself and sequenced to build on skills studied in previous chapters. A language box explains the skill in detail. Go over this explanation as a class and answer any questions. The sub-section concludes with a short listening activity featuring lecture excerpts that focus on the specific note taking skill.

Lecture

Each lecture is divided into two parts, for ease of comprehension. Before they listen, students complete a vocabulary exercise that focuses on the academic vocabulary in the lecture that is likely to be unfamiliar. The vocabulary is presented in the context in which students will hear it; encourage them to guess at the meaning.

Following the vocabulary task, students preview a comprehension task designed to provide a framework for their listening and note taking. The task may involve completing a summary or outline, or answering comprehension questions. Then, students listen to the lecture itself, practicing the note taking skills they have learned. Make it clear to students that for most of the lecture comprehension tasks, their answers need not be word-for-word the same. Encourage them to paraphrase.

After the Lecture

This sub-section invites students to share their perspective through discussion questions that allow them to analyze the chapter content more critically, often by comparing it to new written or graphic material. Students may be asked to apply what they have learned to their own situations. As with other discussion activities included throughout the chapter, this activity will help students prepare for the final oral presentation in two ways: they will develop oral skills and confidence, and they will identify what aspects of the unit content they are most interested in exploring further.

The *Academic Listening and Note Taking* section should take about four or five hours.

Unit Review

This section includes a review of academic vocabulary and unit topics, and culminates in an oral presentation:

Academic Vocabulary Review

The *Academic Vocabulary Review* can be done in class or as homework. As with all vocabulary activities in the book, it stresses the importance of context. As you review the vocabulary words, ask students to recall the context in which they learned them. If a word has been used to mean different things in different chapters (for example, "depressed"), elicit that information as well.

A second vocabulary review activity asks students to answer questions about the unit content; relevant vocabulary words are provided. This activity may be done orally in pairs or small groups. Students may then volunteer sentences to be written on the board, providing a class review of the unit.

Oral Presentation

Each of the unit reviews concludes with a different type of oral presentation. Carefully scaffolded activities, presented in three steps, encourage students to work on oral delivery:

- *Before the Presentation*
- *During the Presentation*
- *After the Presentation*

Before they make their presentations, students are generally instructed to choose or define a topic they will discuss. They may be asked to present to a small or large group, individually or in a team. The organization of the presentation depends on the parameters established in each chapter, but students may be asked to research their topic online or study language related to introducing or structuring a topic. Instructors should monitor the students' choice of topic and make sure they understand how best to structure their allotted time.

The *During the Presentation* section instructs students about speaking clearly, taking time to define new words, using appropriate body language, and other mechanisms for making effective presentations. This is the students' chance to work on their oral delivery and make sure that the audience understands their presentation. This is the instructor's chance to work on oral delivery skills.

After the presentation, students learn to check that their listeners have understood their presentation. They learn language to check for comprehension, engage in self-assessment, and learn how to respond to others' presentations with questions and comments.

The *Unit Review* should take three to four hours of class time, depending on the number of students in the class and the time that instructors decide to dedicate to this activity.

Chapter 1
The Physical Earth

1 Getting Started

1 Reading and thinking about the topic Page 4
B

1. Similarities: Both planets have four seasons, similar landforms, and active volcanoes; Differences: The volcanoes on Mars are much larger than the ones on Earth. Earth has liquid water and a thick atmosphere, but Mars has no liquid water and a very thin atmosphere.
2. Earth's thick atmosphere and liquid water make life possible.

2 Listening to directions Page 4
B

Earth: strong atmosphere, oxygen, liquid water; Both: four seasons, similar landforms, volcanoes; Mars: thin atmosphere, large volcanoes

2 Real-Life Voices

Before the Interviews

1 Understanding word parts Page 5
B

1. geology
2. biology
3. seismograph
4. meteorology
5. volcanologist
6. geography

2 Sharing your knowledge Page 6
A

1. seven, five
2. Asia, Australia
3. Mt. Everest
4. the Dead Sea
5. the Nile
6. the Sahara

Interview 1 – A Geologist Talks

2 Listening for main ideas in an interview Page 7
B

☑ The meaning of geology
☑ The reason Brad became a geologist
☐ The bad points about being a geologist
☑ The project Brad is working on now
☐ Brad's future goals
☑ Brad's feelings about geology

C

Geologists study the Earth's composition (what the Earth is made of) and dynamics (Earth's movement). When Brad was growing up, he asked many questions about the Earth, such as "What causes mountains and earthquakes?" "How do beaches get their shape? Why do the shapes of beaches change?" At his job right now, Brad is measuring the size and shapes of beaches and the amount of erosion at each beach. Brad thinks that geology is fun, important, and exciting.

Interview 2 – Earth's Natural Beauty

2 Listening for details Page 8
B

Main ideas	Details	
	Grand Canyon	Uluru (Ayers Rock)
What it looks like	big – seems to go on forever cliffs – different colors	*large, red rock – looks smooth from far away; up close – rough & has holes*
Its colors	*red, blue, purple, orange, yellow, brown*	reddish-brown can change to pink, purple, gray depending on time of day
The speakers' thoughts and feelings	one of the most beautiful things ever seen; lucky to see it	*it's beautiful*
How it was formed	*formed by water – river eroded rock*	layers of rock were lifted out of the earth; softer rocks eroded – Uluru is what's left

4 Academic Listening and Note Taking

Before the Lecture

1 Listening for main ideas in a lecture Page 11

A

  2   Now, I'd like to discuss each of the three main layers of Earth. First, the crust. . . . There are two kinds of crust: oceanic and continental.

  1   But first, I want to give you some background information about our planet.

  4   Finally, continuing down toward the center of the planet, we come to the core. The core can be divided into two parts: an outer core and an inner core.

  T   Today, let's look inside planet Earth and discuss its internal structure.

  3   Moving down from the crust, the next layer of Earth is called the mantle.

2 Organizing your notes in an outline Page 12

A

Inside Planet Earth
(lecture topic)
I. Background information <u>about the planet</u> (main idea)
II. <u>Crust</u> = Earth's surface layer. Two kinds: (main idea)
A <u>oceanic</u> (subtopic)
B. <u>continental</u> (subtopic)
III. <u>Mantle</u> = next layer down from crust (main idea)
IV. <u>Core</u> = center of planet <u>divided into two parts</u>. (main idea)
A. <u>outer core</u> (subtopic)
B. <u>inner core</u> (subtopic)

Lecture Part 1 – Planet Earth: Background

1 Guessing vocabulary from context Page 13

B

1. e   2. g   3. b   4. a
5. d   6. f   7. c

2 Listening for supporting details Page 14

B

Inside Planet Earth
I. Background information about the planet (main idea)
5   (supporting detail)
1   (supporting detail)
3   (supporting detail)
4   (supporting detail)
2   (supporting detail)

Lecture Part 2 – Inside Our Planet

1 Guessing vocabulary from context Page 15

B

1. f   2. c   3. h   4. g
5. d   6. a   7. b   8. e

2 Listening for supporting details Page 16

B

Inside Planet Earth
II. Crust (main idea)
_7_ (supporting detail)
A. Oceanic (subtopic)
_5_ (supporting detail)
_9_ (supporting detail)
B. Continental (subtopic)
_2_ (supporting detail)
_10_ (supporting detail)
III. Mantle = next layer down from crust (main idea)
_6_ (supporting detail)
_12_ (supporting detail)
_4_ (supporting detail)
IV. Core = center of planet (main idea)
A. Outer core (subtopic)
_8_ (supporting detail)
B. Inner core (subtopic)
_3_ (supporting detail)
_11_ (supporting detail)
_1_ (supporting detail)

After the Lecture

Using your notes to label an illustration Page 17

A

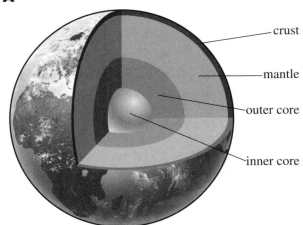

crust

mantle

outer core

inner core

Chapter 2
The Dynamic Earth

1 Getting Started

1 Reading and thinking about the topic Page 19
B

1. Earth's crust is thin, made of hard rock, and broken into many pieces called *plates*.
2. Earth's plates can move away from each other, crash into each other, or rub against each other side by side.
3. Some effects of plate tectonics are volcanoes, earthquakes, and the formation of mountains and valleys.

2 Listening for numerical information about distances and rates Pages 19–20
B

1. The Atlantic Ocean is growing at a rate of about 2.5 cm per year.
2. The Himalaya Mountains are rising at a rate of about 5 mm per year.
3. Two plates in California are moving side by side in opposite directions at a rate of almost 5 cm per year.
4. The Hawaiian Islands are moving northwest toward Japan at a rate of about 7 cm per year.

C

1. 40,000 years
2. 8,850 meters
3. farther apart
4. about 14,286 years

2 Real-Life Voices

Before the Interviews

Interpreting a map Page 21

1. Student responses will vary.
2. Australia.
3. Most volcanoes and earthquakes happen at the edges of the major plates. Tectonic activity happens when the plates push against each other, slide past each other, or move away from each other.

Interview 1 – Living Near an Active Volcano

1 Understanding multiple-choice questions Page 22
B

1. b
2. c
3. a
4. c
5. a

2 Responding to a speaker Page 23
B

1. e
2. c
3. f
4. a
5. d
6. b

Interview 2 – Living with Earthquakes

1 Drawing inferences Page 24
B

1. T
2. F
3. NS
4. T
5. F

2 Retelling what you have heard Page 25

A

1. Zack grew up in San Francisco, and he still lives there now.
2. He usually doesn't notice small earthquakes, so he thinks they are no big deal.
3. He was in a tall building, and he felt like the floor became liquid. He saw the floor and the corners of his office moving like ocean waves.
4. Yoshiko grew up in Tokyo, Japan, and now lives in San Francisco.
5. When an earthquake happens, she first opens the doors and then she moves to a safer spot, such as under a desk or table or into the bathroom. After the earthquake, she meets her family at a designated spot, like a park, school, or other open space.
6. Zack and Yoshiko have an emergency plan in case an earthquake happens. They also keep extra water and other supplies (food, a flashlight, extra batteries, a radio, extra blankets) in their home.

4 Academic Listening and Note Taking

Before the Lecture

1 Building background knowledge on the topic Page 29

B

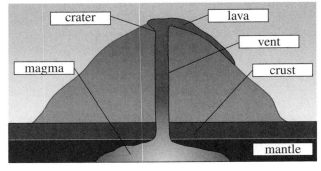

2 Focusing on the introduction Page 30

A

1. *Today's lecture is going to be about*
2. *I'd like to start today's lecture by introducing*
3. *Then I'll describe*
4. *Finally, we'll discuss*

Lecture Part 1 – The Basic Structure of a Volcano

1 Guessing vocabulary from context Page 31

B

1. c   2. d   3. a   4. e   5. b

2 Using telegraphic language Pages 31–32

A

1. Magma comes from ~~Earth's~~ mantle, ~~which is a layer deep below Earth's~~ surface.
2. ~~The~~ upper mantle ~~is from~~ 80 to 150 kilometers below ~~Earth's~~ surface, ~~and the~~ temperatures ~~here are~~ so high ~~that~~ rocks ~~start to~~ melt ~~and~~ become magma.
3. ~~Usually an~~ eruption starts because ~~an~~ earthquake breaks ~~the~~ rock ~~at the~~ top of ~~the~~ mantle ~~and~~ creates ~~an~~ opening.
4. ~~The~~ magma then rises through ~~the~~ opening ~~in the solid rock and~~ moves toward ~~the~~ surface ~~of Earth~~.
5. ~~Finally, the~~ magma comes out ~~of an~~ opening in ~~the~~ crust, ~~called a~~ vent.

C

  3 Magma flows through mantle, pushes against rock
  5 Magma on top of Earth's surface = lava
  1 Volcanoes formed by hot, melted rock (magma) from mantle
  6 Volcano can be gentle (lava flows on surface) or powerful (clouds of ash, rock)
  4 Earthquake breaks rock – magma comes out opening in crust (vent)
  2 Upper mantle 80–150 km below surface; high temperatures melt rock

Lecture Part 2 – Types of Volcanoes

1 Guessing vocabulary from context Page 33

B

1. f   2. a   3. h   4. g
5. d   6. c   7. b   8. e

2 Predicting the content Page 34
B
composite
shield
super volcano

3 Using telegraphic language Page 35
B
Sample notes:

Part 2: Types of Volcanoes
I.   Shield volcanoes
A. Very big
B. Lava flows from vent – gentle _eruptions_
C. _Lava_ cools, becomes hard
Shape like shield: _broad & circular_ , sloping sides
D. Example: Mauna Loa, Hawaii Largest volcano – starts on _sea floor_ , rises to _9,000 m_
II. Composite volcanoes
A. Smaller – 2,500 m
B. Both explosive and gentle eruptions
1. Explosive: layers of _ash & rock_ pile up near _vent_
2. Gentle: Lava flow covers ash, makes _cone_
3. Composite = made up of _different parts_
C. Examples
1. Mt. _Fuji (Japan)_
2. Mt. St. Helens (U.S.)
III. Super volcanoes
A. Biggest volcanoes, most _explosive_ eruptions
B. Don't form _cone_ – leave huge _crater_
C. Don't happen often but can cause _widespread destruction_
D. Example: Toba
1. _70–75,000_ years ago in Indonesia
2. Killed _60% of people_ on Earth
IV. Warning signs before an eruption
A. _Earthquakes_
B. Ground cracks
C. Drinking water _tastes different_
D. _Ice on volcanoes_ starts to melt

After the Lecture
Using your notes to make a study sheet Page 36
A

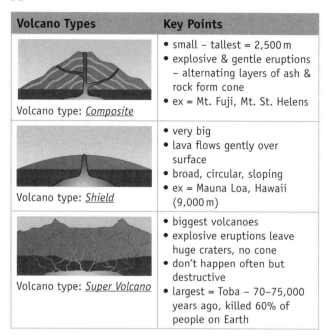

Volcano Types	Key Points
Volcano type: _Composite_	• small – tallest = 2,500 m • explosive & gentle eruptions – alternating layers of ash & rock form cone • ex = Mt. Fuji, Mt. St. Helens
Volcano type: _Shield_	• very big • lava flows gently over surface • broad, circular, sloping • ex = Mauna Loa, Hawaii (9,000 m)
Volcano type: _Super Volcano_	• biggest volcanoes • explosive eruptions leave huge craters, no cone • don't happen often but destructive • largest = Toba – 70–75,000 years ago, killed 60% of people on Earth

Unit 1 Academic Vocabulary Review

A Page 37
1. affect
2. alternating
3. core
4. create
5. energy
6. features
7. internal
8. layer
9. structure
10. percent
11. finally
12. lecture

Chapter 3
Earth's Water Supply

1 Getting Started

1 Reading and thinking about the topic Page 44
B

1. The amount of water on Earth is exactly the same as it was 4.6 billion years ago.
2. Answers may include: water vapor in the atmosphere, clouds, rain, lakes, rivers, oceans, ice, groundwater, water in plants, and water in animals and humans.

2 Building background vocabulary Pages 44–45
A

GAS: cloud, steam
LIQUID: lake, ocean, rain, river, waterfall
SOLID: ice, snow

B

1. ocean	2. rain	3. lake
4. steam	5. ice	6. waterfall

C

1. lake	2. ocean	3. waterfall
4. ice, snow	5. steam	6. rain

2 Real-Life Voices

Before the Interviews

Examining graphic material Pages 46–47
A

1. United States; Cameroon
2. Answers will vary but may include differences in the countries' populations, geography, climates, agricultural practices, industrial development, political conditions, and the lifestyles and daily practices of its people.
3. Student responses will vary.

B

Domestic Use: 13%; Industrial Use: 46%; Agricultural Use: 41%

Interview 1 – Water in the United States

Listening for opinions Page 48
B

Check: 2, 3, 5, 6

Interview 2 – Water in Cambodia

Listening for details Page 49
B

1. _whole country_ People drink mostly surface water.
2. _countryside_ People don't have enough money to buy wood to boil the water.
3. _countryside_ The water has feces in it.
4. _capital city_ People have to buy water from trucks.
5. _whole country_ Thousands of children die from water-borne illnesses every year.
6. _countryside_ The water is very thick, sort of a tea color.

Interview 3 – Water in Cameroon

Listening for specific information Page 50
A

1. Just over a year.
2. At first, she boiled her water or bought bottled water. Later, she did the same thing as other people living in Cameroon.
3. Some parts of Cameroon have good roads and easy access to water, but other parts have bad roads and poor access. People living in the disadvantaged areas have to travel very far to get water.
4. People are hardworking and able to survive under difficult conditions. They are also less wasteful of water.
5. She thinks about the people in Cameroon whenever she turns on her tap or uses water. She thinks differently about water in the world and is more careful not to waste it.

B

Water comes from Earth and flows across Earth. (It's) (like blood). In some cultures, water is seen as (the blood) (of Earth). I think of it that way. The Earth is (like a living) (thing). All the plants and animals are (parts of the Earth's) ("body)." And everything is connected by water. To me, water is a metaphor for life.

3 In Your Own Voice

Page 53

A

1. i	2. d	3. b	4. h	5. j
6. e	7. f	8. g	9. a	10. c

4 Academic Listening and Note Taking

Before the Lecture

1 Predicting the content Page 54

A

4	2
3	1

B

1. c	2. a	3. d	4. b

2 Using symbols and abbreviations Page 55

A

1. g	2. a	3. d	4. i	5. b
6. j	7. h	8. e	9. f	10. c

B

1. Most of E's surf covd in H_2O
2. 97% = salt H_2O ; 3% fr H_2O
3. Of all fresh H_2O: 75% = ice only 25% = liquid
4. <1% H_2O on E = drinking H_2O for all ppl, plants, anim

Lecture Part 1 – Sources of Freshwater

1 Guessing vocabulary from context Page 56

B

1. e	2. g	3. b	4. f
5. a	6. h	7. c	8. d

2 Using symbols and abbreviations Page 57

A

Sample answers

Word	Abbreviation	Word	Abbreviation
enjoyment	*enjymnt*	river	*riv*
flow	*flw*	saltwater	*slt H_2O*
freshwater	*fr H_2O*	stream	*str*
ground	*grnd*	surface	*surf*
industry	*indus*	transportation	*transp*

C

I. Where does fr. H_2O come from?
  A. Rain + snow falls → sinks into *grnd*
  B. If *grnd* is full of H_2O, then stays on *surf*
  C. Small flow of surf water = *str*
  D. If combine, become bigger = *riv*
  C. May form pond / lake, or flow to ocn
II. Functions of fresh H_2O
  A. *riv* carry nutrients + minerals ∴ nearby land rich + fertile
    Farmers also have to give crops *fr H_2O*
  B. Daily tasks, ex. washing dishes + clothes, cleaning, bathing
  C. *indus*
  D. *transp*
  E. Playing + *enjymnt*
  F. *most important = *cln H_2O* for humans + *anim*
    Without *H_2O* life on Earth couldn't exist

Lecture Part 2 – Threats to Earth's Freshwater Supply

1 Guessing vocabulary from context Page 58
B

1. f   2. d   3. b   4. c   5. a   6. e

2 Using bullets and brackets to organize your notes Page 59
B

2. <u>Poll</u>
   - many sources, ex. factories, hum waste + fert
   - poll in air: <u>acid rain</u> falls to E, enters H_2O supply
   - trash enters strm or riv

   } Some H_2O too polluted to use

3. Overuse by humans
   - H_2O cannot ↑ but pop ↑ every yr
   - millions more ppl → <u>use + drink</u> → need for more <u>food</u> → more farming → more <u>H_2O</u> for <u>irrig</u>

   } WWC: > 1 billion ppl, don't have enough safe, clean H_2O

CONCLUSION
   - Ppl can't live more than a few days w/o H_2O
   - Ppl must learn not to waste H_2O
   - All countries must coop to stop <u>poll</u>

   } Humans must learn to use H_2O more carefully

Chapter 4
Earth's Oceans

1 Getting Started

1 Reading and thinking about the topic Page 63
B

1. Seas, bays, and gulfs are smaller than oceans and are partly surrounded by land.
2. All bodies of saltwater are connected, and the same water flows from one area into the other.
3. Only 5% of the world ocean has been explored by scientists; 71% of Earth's surface is covered by ocean water; 99% of Earth's total livable space is in the ocean.

2 Expressing likes and dislikes Page 63
A

1. swimming
2. fishing
3. snorkeling
4. windsurfing
5. sailing

B

1. windsurfing – dislike
2. fishing – like
3. swimming – like
4. snorkeling – dislike
5. sailing – like

2 Real-Life Voices

Before the Interviews

2 Predicting the content Page 65
A

  _T_ 1. It feels like you're sliding over the wave . . . like you're flying through the water.
  _E_ 2. The ocean is very quiet and calm . . . you can just sit there and look at the fish.
  _E_ 3. I often see something or find something interesting.
  _E_ 4. Although there were a couple times when I felt scared . . .
  _T_ 5. You really feel the power of nature, the power of the waves in your whole body.

Interview 1 – Adventure Under the Ocean

Retelling what you have heard Page 66
A

1. When Edmund goes diving, he sometimes finds interesting things in the ocean, like old bottles.
2. One time Edmund saw a sea horse and took a picture of it.
3. Eels have hit Edmund a few times. This was a scary experience for him.
4. One time Edmund saw two whales, a mother and her baby, while he was diving. When the whales heard Edmund, they swam away.

Interview 2 – Surf's Up

1 Listening for main ideas Page 67
B

1. Why did Tomoki start surfing?
✔ He had been interested in the sport since his childhood.
✔ His friend gave him a surfboard.
___ As a child, he spent every summer at the beach, playing in the water.

2. Why does Tomoki love surfing?	
✔ He loves being in the water.	___ He loves being in the sun.
✔ Surfing is challenging.	___ Surfing is easy.
✔ The ocean is beautiful.	✔ Surfing is unique.

3. According to Tomoki, what does a person need to surf well?	
✔ physical fitness	___ very big waves
✔ good balance	___ strong wind
___ a good surfboard	✔ a clean ocean surface

2 Thinking critically about the topic Page 67

A

Edmund and Tomoki think that humans (can /(cannot)) control the ocean.

After the Interviews

Thinking creatively about the topic Page 68

A

1. Tomoki   2. Edmund

4 Academic Listening and Note Taking

Before the Lecture

1 Building background knowledge on the topic Pages 70–71

B

1. The Arctic Ocean is almost completely surrounded by land.
2. The Marianas Trench, the world's deepest place, is located in the Pacific Ocean.
3. The currents in the Indian Ocean change direction during the year, which causes monsoons (strong winds and heavy rains).
4. The Atlantic Ocean is the least salty ocean because many rivers run into it.
5. The Southern Ocean is sometimes called the Antarctic Ocean.
6. The Southern Ocean surrounds the coldest, windiest place on Earth.
7. The Pacific Ocean has more water than all of the other oceans combined.
8. The Atlantic Ocean is slowly growing larger because of plate tectonics.

2 Listening for signal words and phrases Page 72

A

However: showing contrast
Therefore: introducing an effect
As I just said: referring to information mentioned earlier
Consequently: introducing an effect
For example: introducing an example

B

1. However   2. Therefore
3. As I just said   4. Consequently
5. For example

Lecture Part 1 – The World's Oceans

1 Guessing vocabulary from context Page 73

B

1. f   2. g   3. a   4. d
5. c   6. e   7. b

Lecture Part 2 – The Layers of the Ocean

1 Guessing vocabulary from context Page 75

B

1. c   2. d   3. h   4. g
5. b   6. f   7. e   8. a

2 Using handouts to help you take notes Page 76

A

Three main layers:
1. Surface – top 100 to 200 m, sometimes called "the sunlit zone" Warmth and light permeate surface layer Most fish + marine life live here b/c there are many plants to eat
2. Middle – goes to 1,000 m Quick drop in temp, from 17° C at surface to 4° C at 1,000 m weak sunlight = no plants; animals have to swim to surf for food
3. Bottom – below 1,000 m No sunlight, almost freezing temps Animals have spec adaptations, for ex, 1. no eyes   2. give off own light Scientists still don't know much Ocean is last unexplored region on Earth

After the Lecture

Making test questions from your notes Page 77

A

1. The surface layer (sunlit zone), the middle layer, and the bottom layer (midnight zone).
2. Water in the surface layer is relatively warm compared to the bottom layer. The surface layer has an average temperature of 17 degrees Celsius, while the bottom layer has very cold, almost freezing temperatures.
3. There is no sunlight here, and therefore it is pitch black.
4. Surface layer: Most of the ocean's fish and marine life live in this layer. Middle layer: Few animals live in this layer, and they have to swim up to the surface layer to get food. Bottom layer: Animals that live here have to adapt to survive in the dark and cold environment. For example, some fish have no eyes, and others give off their own light.

Unit 2 Academic Vocabulary Review

A Page 78

1. access
2. adapt
3. consequently
4. constantly
5. cooperate
6. environment
7. located
8. region
9. transportation
10. resource

Chapter 5
Earth's Atmosphere

1 Getting Started

1 Reading and thinking about the topic Page 86
B

1. Yes and no. All air on Earth is made of the same gases. However, the quality of air is not the same in all places on Earth.
2. The three factors that affect air quality are:
   1) humidity – how much water is in the air;
   2) particulates – small pieces of dirt, dust, and other matter in the air; and 3) air pressure – how strongly the air presses around us on Earth's surface.

2 Listening for background noise Page 87
B

b	in the countryside
c	at the top of a mountain
d	in a city
a	in a rain forest

C

c	The air is thin.
b	There's a lot of pollen in the air.
a	It is very hot and humid.
d	The air is dirty.

D

a. This person is in a rain forest and is sweating because it is very humid.
b. This person is in the countryside and is sneezing because there's pollen in the air.
c. This person is at the top of a mountain and is gasping because the air is thin.
d. This person is in a city and is coughing because the air is dirty.

2 Real-Life Voices

Before the Interviews

1 Building background knowledge and vocabulary Pages 88–89
A

6	tree pollen	7	airplane
2	car	4	fire
5	wind	3	volcano
1	factory		

B

Natural Sources: tree pollen, wind, volcano, fire
Human-made sources: car, factory, airplane, fire

NOTE: Fires can be categorized as either natural or human-made, depending on how the fire got started. Natural causes include lightning or volcanic eruption; human-made causes include arson or human carelessness.

2 Examining a map Page 89
A

1. The dry regions are mostly located in a band above the equator. The humid regions are above and below the equator, on both sides of the dry regions.
2. Africa is the driest continent. Most of North Africa is dry or very dry.
3. Responses will vary.

Interview 1 – Pollutants in the Air

2 Listening for specific information Page 90
B

Jeff is the director of an environmental organization. He is always thinking about _air quality_ and its effects on _people_ and _nature_. In this interview, Jeff talks about _factors_ that affect air quality, such as _pollutants_ in the air.

C

☑ cars	☐ airplanes	☑ factories	☐ volcanoes
☐ trees	☑ windstorms	☑ wildfire	☐ cigarette smoke

Interview 2 – Air Quality

2 Listening for specific information Page 91

A

1. Shari can't see the *mountains* near her home.
2. The color of the air is *brown*.
3. Shari gets bad *headaches*.
4. It is difficult for Shari to *breathe*.
5. At school, children can't *exercise* outside.

B

1. Smog comes from the words *smoke* and *fog* mixed together.
2. Anytime it's over three or four, they *warn* people to be careful.

Interview 3 – Humid and Dry Air

2 Answering multiple-choice questions Page 92

A

1. b   2. a   3. a   4. a
5. a   6. b   7. b   8. a

4 Academic Listening and Note Taking

Before the Lecture

1 Predicting the content Page 96

A

1. Air is made up of 10 gases.
2. Possible answers include: nitrogen, oxygen, carbon dioxide.
3. Humid.
4. Dry or arid.
5. Particulate matter or particulates.
6. Possible answers: smoggy, hazy, polluted
7. Possible answers: volcanoes, wildfires, windstorms, trees
8. Possible answers: cars, airplanes, factories, wildfires
9. Possible answers: sneezing, coughing, breathing problems, damage to the lungs, headaches, or irritated eyes or throat.

B

The most comfortable level for most people is 50 percent humidity.

C

Sources of humidity mentioned in the lecture are rain, snow, and water vapor from oceans, rivers, trees, plants, and the ground.

2 Identifying key vocabulary in the lecture Page 97

A

1. d   2. b   3. c   4. a

B

1. d   2. a   3. b   4. c

Lecture Part 1 – Humidity

1 Guessing vocabulary from context Page 98

B

1. d   2. a   3. b   4. c

2 Organizing your notes in an outline Page 99

B

The Air We Breathe

I. Gases
  A. Nitrogen makes up *78* %
  B. *Oxygen* makes up 21%
  C. Also *about 10* other gases
II. Water
  A. Vapor is the form of most water in the air
  B. Amount of water in air is called *humidity level*
    1. *80–90* %
      a. high level: lots of water in air
      b. probably feel *uncomfortable*
    2. 50%
      a. *less water in air*
      b. most people feel *comfortable*
    3. *10* %
      a. *deserts* + other dry places
      b. not much water in air
  C. Sources of water
    1. most obvious – liquids or solids that fall from the clouds, e.g., *rain*, *snow*
    2. *oceans* + *rivers*
    3. *trees* + *plants*
    4. *ground*

Lecture Part 2 – Particulate Matter

1 Guessing vocabulary from context Page 100

B

1. e   2. d   3. a   4. h
5. g   6. c   7. f   8. b

2 Organizing your notes in a chart Page 101

B

Types of particulate matter			
Natural		**Human-made**	
Source	**Particles**	**Action**	**Result**
volcano	smoke, ash	*burning wood, plants, or trees*	more particulate matter added to air
forest fire	*smoke*	cut down trees and take water	*easier for dust, dirt to be picked up and carried in the air*
ocean waves	*salt, sand*	*burning coal or other fossil fuels*	pollution added to air
flowers, trees, plants	pollen, natural matter		
environment	*dirt, dust*		

Chapter 6
Weather and Climate

1 Getting Started

1 Reading and thinking about the topic Page 103
B

1. Weather is the condition of the atmosphere at a certain time and place. Climate is the usual weather in an area over many years. The troposphere is the layer of the atmosphere closest to Earth's surface.
2. This statement refers to the climate. It means the area where you live is dry most of the time, even if it rains occasionally.
3. Dry, tropical, mild, variable, polar

2 Understanding scientific symbols Page 103
B

1. rain showers
2. heavy snow
3. fog and rain
4. thunderstorm with hail

3 Listening for specific information Page 104
B

1. The sky is _clear_ and there are no _clouds_. Temperatures are _warm_ here.
2. The sky is _cloudy_. The _wind_ is strong. In about an hour, a _thunderstorm_ will start.
3. The temperature is getting _colder_. Soon the _rain_ will change to _snow_.
4. The heavy _rain_ has ended, but we're still going to have a lot of _fog_ today.

C

1. ○
2. ⚲
   ⚞
3. ●
   ✳
4. ≡

2 Real-Life Voices

Interview 1 – A Future Meteorologist

2 Listening for specific information Page 106
B

Name: Sara
Country of origin: _Portugal_
Major: _meteorology_
Meteorology is the study of _the atmosphere_.

She decided to study meteorology because:

1. _Her father told her science was a good subject to study._
2. _She has always been fascinated with the sky._

C

Earth is like _a big aquarium_ …
.. we're just like _fish_ …
… our atmosphere is just like _water_.

Interview 2 – Severe Weather

2 Predicting the content Pages 107–108
B

Dorothy was in a _blizzard_.
Yukiya got caught in a _flood_.
Evylynn experienced a _hurricane_.

D

E	1.	. . . trees and lampposts were flying everywhere.
E	2.	Once you experience something like that, you remember it for the rest of your life.
E	3.	Houses right across the street from me were torn apart.
Y	4.	I actually saw one car floating!
D	5.	. . . the weight of the snow brought down a lot of tree branches.
Y	6.	I was like, "This is definitely going to be on the news!"
D	7.	. . . it was falling very fast, and by Friday morning we had about two feet of it.

3 Listening for opinions Page 108

Do you think that global warming is affecting the weather on Earth?		Reasons for opinion
Sara	YES / NO / (DON'T KNOW)	*Some changes may be caused by humans, but others may be natural. With science, until you have the right answer, you don't know for sure.*
Dorothy	(YES) / NO / DON'T KNOW	*Recent changes in the weather are not part of the natural cycle. For example, hurricanes are stronger and winters are warmer than they used to be.*
Yukiya	(YES) / NO / DON'T KNOW	*Global warming is melting the ice in Antarctica. This is causing the ocean level to rise, which causes more hurricanes.*
Evylynn	(YES) / NO / DON'T KNOW	*Global warming is making the weather worse and increasing the risk of dangerous weather. Humans are changing Earth, and these changes affect the weather.*

4 Academic Listening and Note Taking

Before the Lecture

1 Building background knowledge on the topic Page 111
B

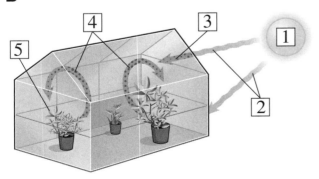

2 Listening for numerical information Page 112
B

1. 4.6 billion years
2. Thirty-five percent
3. 1 degree centigrade
4. Eighty percent

Lecture Part 1 – The Greenhouse Effect

1 Guessing vocabulary from context Page 112
B

1. d   2. b   3. c   4. a   5. e

2 Copying a lecturer's illustrations Page 113
B

  3   a. Seventy percent passes through the atmosphere.

  7   b. Most of the warmth emitted by the Earth stays in our atmosphere.

  4   c. Half of that energy reaches the Earth's surface.

  2   d. Thirty percent of the sun's energy is reflected off the atmosphere.

  6   e. About ten percent of that energy is leaked back into space.

  1   f. Energy from the sun approaches the Earth.

  5   g. The Earth emits the sun's warmth back toward space.

C

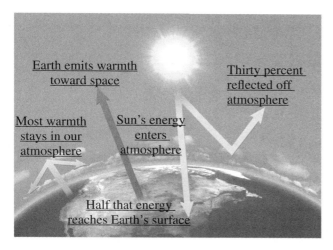

Earth emits warmth toward space

Thirty percent reflected off atmosphere

Most warmth stays in our atmosphere

Sun's energy enters atmosphere

Half that energy reaches Earth's surface

Lecture Part 2 – Effects of Global Warming

1 Guessing vocabulary from context Page 114

B

1. e   2. a   3. b   4. d   5. c

2 Listening for cause and effect Page 115

A

1. "Some of this rise is due to the heating of the ocean surface. When ocean waters warm, they expand, or get bigger, and so the sea level rises."
2. "The melt water is entering the ocean and resulting in a rise in sea level."
3. "Changes in the weather are another consequence of global warming."
4. "Hurricanes develop over warm oceans, and so the rise in ocean temperatures may cause more and perhaps stronger hurricanes."

B

1. oceans warm → oceans exp (get bigger) → sea lev ↑
2. melt H$_2$O enters ocean → sea lev ↑
3. glob warm → chngs in weather
4. ↑ ocean temps → more & strngr hurr

Unit 3 Academic Vocabulary Review

A Page 117

1. debatable
2. expand
3. global
4. individually
5. maintain
6. Obviously
7. consequence
8. release
9. composed
10. prediction
11. absorb
12. define

Chapter 7
Plants and Animals

1 Getting Started

1 Reading and thinking about the topic Page 126
B

1. Scientists have identified more than 1.8 million animal species and more than 300,000 plant species on Earth.
2. Plants and animals move, grow, use food and water to make energy, react to their environments, reproduce, and are interconnected with each other.

2 Listening for specific information Pages 126–127
A

1. platypus
2. bamboo
3. Goliath beetle
4. Venus flytrap
5. blue whale
6. giant sequoia tree

C

Organism	Interesting facts	Habitat (where it lives)
1. blue whale	largest animal in the world; *can be 33 m long, 150 tons heart = size of small car*	deep oceans
2. Venus flytrap	eats meat; catches insects	*originally the U.S. but now grows all over world*
3. platypus	has bill and webbed feet like duck but has wide, flat tail; *lives on land but is good swimmer*	*only Australia*
4. giant sequoia tree	*largest type of tree on Earth; can be more than 100m tall*	*California*
5. Goliath beetle	*largest & heaviest insect on Earth*	*everywhere except for ocean and cold polar regions*
6. *bamboo*	*type of grass; fastest growing plant on Earth – can grow 4cm/hour*	*many different habitats, from cold mountains to hot, tropical jungles*

2 Real-Life Voices

Before the Interviews

2 Building background knowledge on the topic Page 128
B

a. The ostrich has excellent eyesight, but a poor sense of smell and hearing; the zebra has an excellent sense of smell and hearing, but poor eyesight. The two animals travel together and warn each other of danger.
b. The clownfish hides in the sea anemone and is protected from predators; the sea anemone eats fish that the clownfish attracts.
c. The plover cleans food from the crocodile's teeth and eats the food.
d. The honeybee eats the nectar of a flower; it spreads pollen so the flower can reproduce.

Interview 1 – A Green Thumb

2 Listening for specific information Page 129
B

	Frank	Vickie
How he or she became interested in gardening	When he was a kid, everybody *had gardens and planted vegetables*.	When she was younger, everyone was trying to *be green and natural by growing their own food*.
Favorite kind of plant to grow now	He likes to grow *native* plants.	She likes to grow *perennials*, which are plants that come back year after year.
What he or she likes about plants and gardening	He likes the *challenge* of finding and collecting the plants.	It helps her forget *day-to-day troubles*. It also makes her feel *connected* to the earth.

Interview 2 – The Galapagos Islands

2 Listening for examples Page 131
A and B

1. You don't have to go far before you see wildlife.
   (For example, / For instance,) → d. on the day I
   arrived . . . I saw Galapagos sea lions right away. I'd
   been there only 20 minutes and I saw sea lions.
2. . . . I saw a lot of birds. Many different kinds of birds,
   (such as / like) → a. blue-footed boobies, red-footed
   boobies, albatross . . . also pelicans, flamingos,
   and penguins.
3. There's been a lot of environmental damage already,
   so the idea that it's an untouched environment is
   wrong. (Let me give you an example: / For example,)
   → b. there used to be 13 subspecies of Galapagos
   giant tortoises, but now two are extinct.
4. . . . any ecosystem is so closely connected that even
   one small thing can change the balance and destroy
   the system. (For example, / For instance,) → c. there's
   a tree that one kind of bird uses for food and shelter. If
   you cut down the tree, you lose the bird, too.

After the Interviews

1 Examining graphic material Page 132
B

1. Plants had the most threatened species in 2000 as well
   as in 2012.
2. Plants had the greatest increase in threatened species
   between 2000 and 2012 (3,582 more threatened
   species in 2012 than in 2000). However, amphibians
   had the greatest percentage increase in number of
   threatened species. Some reasons for the increased
   number of threatened species are loss of habitat,
   changes to the water supply, climate change, invasive
   species that serve as competitors or predators, and
   human disturbance. No group had fewer threatened
   species in 2012 than in 2000, but mammals
   remained relatively stable, perhaps due to increased
   conservation efforts.
3. Student responses will vary.
4. Student responses will vary.

4 Academic Listening and Note Taking

Before the Lecture

1 Previewing the topic Page 135
C

Excretion: removal of waste materials from a living
organism (separating waste from the body)
Movement: change from one place or position to another
Reproduction: the process of making more of the
same organism
Sensitivity: feeling and reacting to the environment
Growth: increase in size
Nutrition: the process of getting food
Respiration: the process of changing food into energy
by using oxygen (animals get the oxygen they need
by breathing)

2 Listening for expressions of contrast Page 136
A and C

1. Plants, for example, grow taller and wider throughout
   their lives. Animals start growing as soon as they
   are born. (Unlike plants,) however, they usually stop
   growing when they become adults.
2. I'm sure you can think of many examples of different
   kinds of animal movement . . . Plants move, too, (but)
   but not in the same way as animals.
3. Plants have a very special way of getting food – they
   make it themselves. . . . Animals, (on the other hand,)
   cannot make their own food.
4. The process of respiration helps to change food into
   energy. Now, animals take in oxygen by breathing in
   air, (whereas) plants take in oxygen through tiny holes
   in their leaves.
5. During reproduction, plants and animals make more
   of their own kind. Animals have babies or lay eggs.
   (In contrast,) most plants make seeds, which fall onto
   the soil and grow into new plants.

Lecture Part 1 – Growth, Movement, and Sensitivity

1 Guessing vocabulary from context Page 137
B

1. g 2. c 3. a 4. b
5. f 6. e 7. d

2 Checking your notes Pages 138–139
B

Life process	Plants	Animals
Growth (size ↑)	Grow taller and wider t/out life	Start at birth Stop growing ~~when they die~~ *when adults*
Movement	– move roots ↓ e, stems + lvs ↑ to sky – flwrs open + close – ~~faster~~ *slower* than anim mvmt	Ex walk, fly, swim, etc.
	Both P + A move to get food, safe place to live, esc from danger	
Sensitivity (notice envir; respond to changes in envir)	– ~~more~~ *fewer* senses than anim – react to stimuli, ex H_2O, light – sunflwr follows ~~moon~~ *sun*	– Senses: see, hear, smell, taste, ~~talk~~ *feel* – Use to get info + react to envir

Lecture Part 2 – Nutrition, Respiration, Excretion, and Reproduction

1 Guessing vocabulary from context Page 139
B

1. e 2. f 3. d 4. b 5. a 6. c

2 Organizing your notes in a chart Page 140
B

Life process	Plants	Animals
Nutrition (getting food)	– CO_2 + H_2O + sunlight = food – Stored in plnt, used when plnt needs energy	– *cannot make own food* – *∴ eat plnts, other anim*
Respiration (food → energy using O_2)	– *get O_2 thru holes in lvs*	– *get O_2 by breathing*
Excretion (remove waste)	– *thru lvs, roots*	– breath, sweat, urine, excrement
Reproduction (make more of own kind, nec to cont species)	– *seeds*	– *babies* – *eggs*

After the Lecture

Applying what you have learned Page 141
A

	1. Automobile	2. Sunflower	3. Fire	4. Student's own idea
Movement	✓	✓	✓	
Growth	✗	✓	✓	
Sensitivity	✓	✓	✓	
Nutrition	✓	✓	✓	
Respiration	✗	✓	✓	
Excretion	✓	✓	✓	
Reproduction	✗	✓	✗	
Living?	Y /Ⓝ	Ⓨ/ N	Y /Ⓝ	Y / N

C

1. growth, movement
2. sensitivity, movement, nutrition
3. respiration, excretion
4. sensitivity, movement, nutrition

Chapter 8
Humans

1 Getting Started

1 Reading and thinking about the topic Page 143
B

1. Three examples of systems mentioned in the passage are the system that helps us process food, the system that helps us breathe, and the system that helps us move.
2. Student responses will vary.

2 Listening to directions Pages 143–144
A

Task 1 b
Task 2 Answers will vary
Task 3 Answers will vary

C

Task 1 __2__
Task 2 __3__
Task 3 __1__

2 Real-Life Voices

Before the Interviews

2 Building background knowledge on the topic Page 146
B

1. Swimming: a, b, d
2. Weight training: a, d
3. Bicycling: a, b, d
4. Yoga: a, c
5. Push-ups: a, d
6. Jogging: a, b, d

Interview 1 – Running Track

Listening for main ideas Page 147
C

__2__ brings in more oxygen for the muscles
__4__ helps the body remember the best positions for running
__3__ builds up the lungs
__2, 3__ makes the heart stronger
__1, 5__ builds muscle strength
__2__ helps you breathe better

Interview 2 – Eat to Live, Don't Live to Eat

2 Listening for specific information Pages 148–149
B

1. __c__ Fiber
2. __f__ Protein
3. __b__ Carbohydrates
4. __d__ Fat
5. __e__ Calcium
6. __a__ Vitamin D

After the Interviews

2 Considering related information Page 150

A

1. Vegetables provide many health benefits. Most vegetables are naturally low in fat and calories, and none have cholesterol. Vegetables are important sources of many nutrients, including fiber and vitamins.

   Grains are important sources of many nutrients. In addition, grains may help reduce cholesterol levels and lower risk of heart disease, diabetes, and other chronic diseases.

2. Proteins are the building blocks for bones, muscles, skin, and blood. However, some foods in the protein group are high in saturated fats, so these foods should be limited. Fruits are naturally low in fat, sodium, and calories and are important sources of essential nutrients. They are high in vitamins–and in sugar as well. They lack some of the long-lasting forms of energy contained in proteins and grains.

3. Usually dairy products are not part of a main meal. Milk, cheese, and butter are used to prepare food and as a condiment.

4. Student responses will vary.

4 Academic Listening and Note Taking

Before the Lecture

1 Building background knowledge on the topic Pages 152–153

A

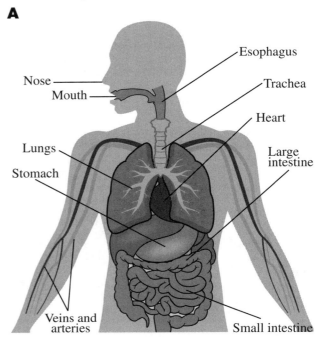

B

1. The esophagus connects the mouth to the stomach. Food travels down the esophagus to the stomach during digestion.

   The heart is the source of power for the cardiovascular system. It pumps blood through the entire body.

   The large intestine absorbs water from food during digestion. The water goes into the body, and the remaining waste in the intestine is removed from the body by excretion.

   The lungs are where oxygen from inhaled air passes into the body, and carbon dioxide (waste produced during cell activity) passes from the body into the lungs, to be exhaled in our breath.

   The mouth takes in air during the process of respiration and helps break down food during the process of digestion.

   The nose brings air into the body during respiration; it is also the primary organ for the sense of smell.

   The small intestine absorbs nutrients from digested food and passes them into the blood.

   The stomach is where food is broken down so that the body can absorb water and nutrients from the food.

   The trachea connects the mouth and nose to the lungs and serves as a passage for inhaled and exhaled air.

   The veins and arteries carry blood back and forth between the body and the heart.

2. The nose, trachea, lungs, and mouth are part of the respiratory system. The large intestine, esophagus, mouth, small intestine, and stomach are part of the digestive system. The arteries, veins, and heart are part of the cardiovascular system.

2 Listening for expressions of time order Page 153

B

1. This phase can last for several hours, and _when_ it's over, the food has become a thick soup.
2. From the stomach, it _then_ moves into the small intestine, where something very important happens.
3. _After_ taking all of the nutrients out of the food, the body doesn't need the leftover food anymore.
4. When we breathe, air enters our body through our mouth and nose. _Next_, it travels through an airway into our lungs.
5. _Finally_, the blood returns to the heart, ready to begin the cycle all over again.

Lecture Part 1 – The Digestive System

1 Guessing vocabulary from context Page 154

B

1. a	2. e	3. g	4. h	5. i
6. c	7. f	8. d	9. b	

2 Taking notes in a flowchart Page 155

B

Digestive System

- body uses energy in food
- proc of bkng down food, releasing nutr into body = digestion

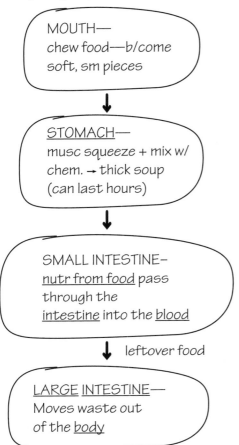

MOUTH—
chew food—b/come
soft, sm pieces

↓

STOMACH—
musc squeeze + mix w/
chem. → thick soup
(can last hours)

↓

SMALL INTESTINE—
<u>nutr from food</u> pass
through the
<u>intestine</u> into the <u>blood</u>

↓ leftover food

<u>LARGE</u> <u>INTESTINE</u>—
Moves waste out
of the <u>body</u>

whole proc ~ <u>24</u> hrs

Lecture Part 2 – The Respiratory and Cardiovascular Systems

1 Guessing vocabulary from context Page 156

B

1. b	2. e	3. d	4. f	5. h
6. g	7. i	8. a	9. c	

2 Taking notes in a flowchart Page 157

C

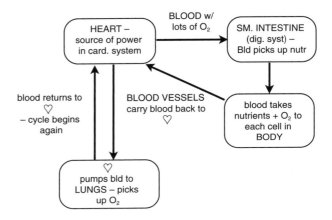

Cardiovascular Syst. = blood, ♡, blood vessels

HEART – source of power in card. system

BLOOD w/ lots of O_2

SM. INTESTINE (dig. syst) – Bld picks up nutr

blood takes nutrients + O_2 to each cell in BODY

BLOOD VESSELS carry blood back to ♡

blood returns to ♡ – cycle begins again

♡ pumps bld to LUNGS – picks up O_2

Unit 4 Academic Vocabulary Review

A Page 159

1. cycle
2. functional
3. identification
4. similarly
5. survival
6. Finally
7. react
8. challenging
9. diversity
10. maintain

Chapter 1 • Lecture Quiz

Part 1 True/False questions (50 points)

Decide if the following statements are true (T) or false (F).

_____ 1. Earth is made up of three main layers.

_____ 2. Earth is the largest planet in the solar system.

_____ 3. In general, Earth's temperature increases as you go down from the surface toward the center of the planet.

_____ 4. The main topic of this lecture is the difference between Earth and the other planets.

Part 2 Multiple choice questions (50 points)

Circle the best answer from the choices listed.

1. Earth is the _____ planet from the sun.

    a. 1st

    b. 3rd

    c. 5th

    d. 8th

2. Scientists use _____ to learn about Earth's internal structure.

    a. ocean waves

    b. seismic waves

    c. liquid rock

    d. fruit

3. Most of Earth's surface is covered by _____.

    a. forests

    b. layers

    c. continental crust

    d. oceanic crust

4. _____ is thicker than oceanic crust.

    a. continental crust

    b. the mantle

    c. the core

    d. all of the above

5. The upper part of the mantle is _____.

   a. hot and soft

   b. cool and solid

   c. made of iron and nickel

   d. under high pressure

6. The mantle is about _____ kilometers thick.

   a. 6–11

   b. 30–40

   c. 2,900

   d. 13,000

7. A unique feature of _____ is that it has liquid rock.

   a. the outer core

   b. the inner core

   c. the crust

   d. Mars

8. The hottest part of Earth is the _____.

   a. crust

   b. upper mantle

   c. lower mantle

   d. inner core

Chapter 2 • Lecture Quiz

Part 1 True/False questions (50 points)

Decide if the following statements are true (T) or false (F).

_____ 1. There are about 75 volcanoes on the surface of Earth.

_____ 2. Volcanoes usually erupt suddenly, without giving any warning signs.

_____ 3. Dr. Fryer doesn't like volcanoes because they are scary.

_____ 4. Dr. Fryer talks about three basic types of volcanoes in her lecture.

Part 2 Multiple choice questions (50 points)

Circle the best answer from the choices listed.

1. Liquid rock on the surface of Earth is called _____.

    a. magma

    b. ash

    c. vent

    d. lava

2. Volcanic eruptions are usually started by _____.

    a. pressure

    b. gases

    c. high temperatures

    d. earthquakes

3. An opening in the Earth's crust is called _____.

    a. a vent

    b. an explosion

    c. the mantle

    d. an earthquake

4. An example of a shield volcano is _____.

    a. Toba

    b. Hawaii

    c. Mauna Loa

    d. Mt. Fuji

5. Composite volcanoes have _____.

   a. a broad, circular shape

   b. alternating layers

   c. the most explosive eruptions

   d. all of the above

6. When the Toba volcano erupted, _____.

   a. 75,000 people died

   b. more than half of the people on Earth ended

   c. all life on Earth ended

   d. a big, cone-shaped volcano was formed

7. The least dangerous type of volcano is probably the _____ volcano.

   a. shield

   b. composite

   c. super

   d. Mt. St. Helens

8. Dr. Fryer mentions all of the following warning signs except _____.

   a. cracks in the ground

   b. loud noises

   c. melting ice

   d. the taste of drinking water

Photocopiable

Chapter 3 • Lecture Quiz

Part 1 True/False questions (50 points)

Decide if the following statements are true (T) or false (F).

_____ 1. Most of the water covering Earth's surface is drinking water.

_____ 2. According to the lecture, farms are located near rivers so that the animals can drink the water.

_____ 3. The most serious problem affecting Earth's water supply is overuse by humans.

_____ 4. The lecturer believes all people must work together to protect Earth's water supply.

Part 2 Multiple choice questions (50 points)

Circle the best answer from the choices listed.

1. The main topic of this lecture is _____ water.

    a. salt

    b. ice

    c. surface

    d. ground

2. _____ of water on Earth is freshwater in liquid form.

    a. Less than 1 percent

    b. About 3 percent

    c. About 25 percent

    d. About 75 percent

3. Water usually stays on Earth's surface when _____.

    a. the ground is already full of water

    b. there is a path cut into the land

    c. two streams combine into a river

    d. it is snowing

4. Water carries a lot of _____, which can help make land more _____.

    a. salt, fertile

    b. pollution, rich

    c. nutrients, dry

    d. nutrients, fertile

5. Washing dishes, washing clothes, and bathing are all examples of _____.

    a. overuse of water

    b. transportation

    c. farming activities

    d. daily tasks

6. The lecturer discusses all of the following threats to water except _____.

    a. land development

    b. pollution

    c. global warming

    d. overuse by humans

7. Air pollution can come from _____.

    a. factories

    b. trash

    c. fertilizers

    d. all of the above

8. The problems discussed in the lecture are caused by _____.

    a. animals

    b. humans

    c. nature

    d. all of the above

Chapter 4 • Lecture Quiz

Part 1 True/False questions (50 points)

Decide if the following statements are true (T) or false (F).

_____ 1. Most of Earth's oceans are located in the southern half of the planet.

_____ 2. The biggest and deepest ocean is located between Europe and North America.

_____ 3. The largest layer of the ocean is the middle layer.

_____ 4. As you go down into the ocean, the temperature and light decrease.

Part 2 Multiple choice questions (50 points)

Circle the best answer from the choices listed.

1. _____ percent of the Earth's surface is covered by ocean.

    a. 29

    b. 61

    c. 71

    d. 80

2. The northernmost ocean is the _____ ocean.

    a. Pacific

    b. Atlantic

    c. Indian

    d. Arctic

3. All oceans on Earth are _____.

    a. deep

    b. connected

    c. dense

    d. pitch black

4. Which of the following is NOT true of the surface layer?

    a. Its nickname is the "sunlit zone."

    b. Many fish live there.

    c. It is very dense.

    d. Its average temperature is 17°C.

Photocopiable

5. Animals swim from the middle layer to the surface layer _____.

    a. to find food

    b. because they like warm temperatures

    c. for exercise

    d. because they don't have eyes

6. The midnight zone begins around _____ meters deep.

    a. 100

    b. 200

    c. 1,000

    d. 3,800

7. Water temperature changes most quickly in the _____.

    a. surface layer

    b. middle layer

    c. bottom layer

    d. middle and bottom layers

8. The lecturer talks about all of the following topics except _____.

    a. threats to Earth's oceans

    b. water temperature

    c. ocean structure

    d. marine life

Name: _____

Date: _____

Chapter 5 • Lecture Quiz

Part 1 True/False questions (50 points)

Decide if the following statements are true (T) or false (F).

_____ 1. According to this lecture, the air is empty.

_____ 2. Nitrogen and oxygen together make up 99 percent of the air.

_____ 3. A humidity level of 10 percent means there is not much water in the air.

_____ 4. All particulate matter in the air is caused by human activity.

Part 2 Multiple choice questions (50 points)

Circle the best answer from the choices listed.

1. There are _____ gases in the air.

   a. 10

   b. 12

   c. 21

   d. 78

2. Gases that make up the air sometimes have a strong _____.

   a. color

   b. smell

   c. taste

   d. none of the above

3. The amount of water vapor in the air is called _____.

   a. humidity

   b. rain

   c. gas

   d. sticky

4. All of the following are mentioned as sources of water in the air except _____.

   a. humans

   b. clouds

   c. plants

   d. the ground

5. Particulate matter is tiny pieces of _____ that float in the air.

   a. gas

   b. liquid matter

   c. solid matter

   d. vapor

6. The lecturer discusses two kinds of particulate matter, natural and _____.

   a. active

   b. man-made

   c. volcanic

   d. solid

7. If your nose starts itching when you smell some flowers, it is probably caused by _____.

   a. salt

   b. dirt

   c. pollen

   d. wind

8. The lecturer's main message is: People should _____.

   a. move to humid areas

   b. avoid particulate matter

   c. not burn fossil fuels

   d. think about what is in the air

Photocopiable

Name: _____

Date: _____

Chapter 6 • Lecture Quiz

Part 1 True/False questions (50 points)

Decide if the following statements are true (T) or false (F).

_____ 1. Greenhouse gases have always been a part of Earth's atmosphere.

_____ 2. Earth's average surface temperature has doubled in the past 100 years.

_____ 3. The lecturer believes that global warming is caused by an increase in the greenhouse effect.

_____ 4. The lecturer believes it is too late to stop global warming.

Part 2 Multiple choice questions (50 points)

Circle the best answer from the choices listed.

1. Greenhouse gases cause the atmosphere to _____.

    a. mix

    b. move

    c. expand

    d. warm up

2. About _____ percent of the energy that comes from the sun enters Earth's atmosphere.

    a. 10

    b. 30

    c. 35

    d. 70

3. Greenhouse gases stop heat energy from _____.

    a. entering the ocean

    b. returning to space

    c. being absorbed by Earth

    d. staying in the atmosphere

4. In the past 100 years, the greenhouse effect has become stronger because of _____.

    a. human activity

    b. rising sea level

    c. global warming

    d. the sun

5. _____ is not mentioned as a possible cause of the rising sea level.

    a. Ocean expansion

    b. Change in the weather

    c. Melting snow

    d. Warmer ocean temperature

6. In the past 40 years, _____ have doubled.

    a. areas experiencing drought

    b. changes in the weather

    c. stronger hurricanes

    d. melting ice and snow

7. According to the lecture, the sea level may rise another _____ centimeters in the twenty-first century.

    a. 3

    b. 15–25

    c. 60

    d. 80

8. The lecturer implies that the main cause of global warming is _____.

    a. scientific studies

    b. use of greenhouse gases

    c. use of fossil fuels

    d. all of the above

Chapter 7 • Lecture Quiz

Part 1 True/False questions (50 points)

Decide if the following statements are true (T) or false (F).

_____ 1. Scientists are not sure how to check if something is living or nonliving.

_____ 2. Both plants and animals have the same reasons for moving.

_____ 3. Plants directly or indirectly provide food for all animals on Earth.

_____ 4. According to the lecturer, a car is a living thing because it performs all seven life processes.

Part 2 Multiple choice questions (50 points)

Circle the best answer from the choices listed.

1. If something is missing one of the seven life processes, it is considered to be _____.

   a. nonliving

   b. living

   c. sensitive

   d. special

2. Plant movement is _____ than animal movement.

   a. wider

   b. taller

   c. slower

   d. stranger

3. All of the following are reasons for animal movement except _____.

   a. getting food

   b. making food

   c. finding a place to live

   d. running away from danger

4. Animals use their _____ to gather information about their environment.

   a. senses

   b. energy

   c. reaction

   d. growth

5. The lecturer talks about the sunflower as an example of the process of _____.

    a. movement

    b. sensitivity

    c. nutrition

    d. growth

6. Because all organisms need energy, _____ are especially important processes.

    a. growth and movement

    b. nutrition and respiration

    c. respiration and reproduction

    d. nutrition and excretion

7. Animals get oxygen _____.

    a. by eating plants

    b. through tiny holes

    c. by changing food into energy

    d. by breathing

8. The purpose of reproduction is to _____.

    a. get rid of waste materials

    b. enjoy time with children

    c. grow old and die

    d. continue the species

Chapter 8 • Lecture Quiz

Part 1 True/False questions (50 points)

Decide if the following statements are true (T) or false (F).

_____ 1. The digestive system, the respiratory system, and the cardiovascular system work together to bring oxygen and nutrients to all parts of the human body.

_____ 2. A group of organs that work together to carry out a specific function is called a "body system."

_____ 3. The main topic of this lecture is the 11 systems of the human body.

_____ 4. The lecturer feels that the digestive, respiratory, and cardiovascular systems are the three most important systems in the human body.

Part 2 Multiple choice questions (50 points)

Circle the best answer from the choices listed.

1. There are _____ human body systems.

    a. one

    b. three

    c. seven

    d. eleven

2. Food is important for the body because it _____.

    a. contains oxygen

    b. contains nutrients

    c. tastes delicious

    d. is always healthy

3. The correct order in digestion is _____.

    a. mouth, stomach, small intestine

    b. mouth, stomach, blood

    c. stomach, large intestine, small intestine

    d. none of the above

4. Nutrients become part of the cardiovascular system in the _____.

    a. mouth

    b. stomach

    c. small intestine

    d. large intestine

5. The mouth is part of the _____ system.

    a. digestive

    b. respiratory

    c. both a and b

    d. neither a nor b

6. The most important function of the respiratory system is to bring _____ into the body.

    a. food

    b. blood

    c. exercise

    d. oxygen

7. Blood goes to the small intestine in order to get _____.

    a. waste

    b. nutrients

    c. fresh oxygen

    d. cells

8. It takes _____ for blood to travel around the entire body.

    a. about 20 seconds

    b. a few minutes

    c. 8 minutes

    d. about 20 minutes

Photocopiable

Lecture Quiz Answer Keys

Chapter 1
PART 1
1. T
2. F
3. T
4. F
PART 2
1. b
2. b
3. d
4. d
5. b
6. c
7. a
8. d

Chapter 2
PART 1
1. F
2. F
3. F
4. T
PART 2
1. d
2. d
3. a
4. c
5. b
6. b
7. a
8. b

Chapter 3
PART 1
1. F
2. F
3. T
4. T
PART 2
1. c
2. a
3. a
4. d
5. d
6. c
7. d
8. b

Chapter 4
PART 1
1. T
2. F
3. F
4. T
PART 2
1. c
2. d
3. b
4. c
5. a
6. c
7. b
8. a

Chapter 5
PART 1
1. F
2. T
3. T
4. F
PART 2
1. b
2. d
3. a
4. a
5. c
6. b
7. c
8. d

Chapter 6
PART 1
1. T
2. F
3. T
4. F
PART 2
1. d
2. d
3. b
4. a
5. b
6. a
7. c
8. c

Chapter 7
PART 1
1. F
2. T
3. T
4. F
PART 2
1. a
2. c
3. b
4. a
5. b
6. b
7. d
8. d

Chapter 8
PART 1
1. T
2. T
3. F
4. F
PART 2
1. d
2. b
3. a
4. c
5. c
6. d
7. b
8. a

Audio Script

◄)) **Unit 1: Planet Earth**
CD1
TR02 **Chapter 1: The Physical Earth**

Getting Started:

Listening to directions, page 4

Look at the diagram. There is a large circle on the left. It is labeled "Earth." There is another, smaller circle on the right. This circle is labeled "Mars." Next to the circle on the left, write about some of Earth's features. Next to the circle on the right, write about the features of Mars. It's all right to use single words or simple phrases. You don't have to write complete sentences. In the middle part of the diagram, under where the two circles overlap, write about the features that Earth and Mars have in common.

◄)) **Interview 1: A Geologist Talks**
CD1
TR03 **Listening for main ideas in an interview, page 7**

Interviewer: Brad, you're a geologist. Can you define "geology" for me?

Brad: Well, the simplest way to define geology is the study of rocks. But there's a little more to it than that. It's really the study of the composition and dynamics of Earth, from its center to its surface

Interviewer: The composition and dynamics of Earth. OK, so "composition" is like, what Earth is composed of, or made up of, right?

Brad: Right! And "dynamics" refers to Earth's movement. So, geologists study what Earth is made up of and how it moves.

Interviewer: How did you become interested in geology?

Brad: I guess I've always had all these questions about Earth. Like, the first time I saw the Rocky Mountains, these huge mountains, I had so many questions in my head: How could these mountains be here? What caused this? And when we had an earthquake in California I asked: Why is Earth shaking? When I was growing up, I was always interested in beaches: How do beaches get their shape, and why do they change? So, I've always been really interested in why things look the way they do. And I've always wanted to know why things change on our planet.

Interviewer: It sounds like from a young age you had questions about Earth. So it sounds like geology is a very good career for you.

Brad: Yes. I enjoy studying geology and I love my work.

Interviewer: What are you working on right now?

Brad: Now, we go to beaches and measure the size and shape of each beach. We measure the size and shape at different seasons and from year to year. Then we see if the beaches are changing shape over time.

Interviewer: And have you found that the shape of the beaches is changing?

Brad: There's definitely change. The shape of the beaches changes every year, between the winter and summer months. But what we're really looking for is a long-term erosion problem.

Interviewer: Long-term erosion — does that mean the beaches are eroding more and more over time?

Brad: That's right. If the beaches don't come back year after year, that's not a temporary change. It's a trend. In other words, the beaches are eroding.

Interviewer: So, Brad, tell me, why should people care about geology?

Brad: First of all, it's just a lot of fun. You get to work outdoors. But second of all, it's important to our society. Humans are having a big effect on our planet, and it's important to understand what we're doing to Earth. So people should be excited about geology because it's fun, and because it's important for our future.

◄)) **Interview 2: Earth's Natural Beauty**
CD1
TR04 **Listening for details, page 8**

Interviewer: So, Gaby, you've been to the Grand Canyon two times?

Gaby: Yes. The first time I went to the Grand Canyon, I went hiking and camping there. The second time I got to ride in a helicopter and fly down into the canyon.

Interviewer: The Grand Canyon is a very popular place to visit in America, right?

Gaby: Definitely! I think the Grand Canyon is America's most famous natural landmark.

Interviewer: What does it look like?

Gaby: Well, it's really, really big. When you stand there looking at it, it seems to go on forever. And there are cliffs that are all different colors, like red and blue, purple and orange, yellow and brown. It almost looks like a painter came and just painted the sides of the canyon with all these different colors.

Interviewer: I'm surprised to hear that. I thought it wouldn't have much color, since it's formed out of rock.

Gaby: I thought so, too, but the cool thing is the colors of the rocks are so different. And when the sun moves, it changes the colors of the canyon walls. So if you stand there for an hour, you can see the light changing as it moves across the rocks.

Interviewer: Interesting! So the changing light makes the rocks look different?

Gaby: Yes, the same area looks totally different when the light changes.

Interviewer: It sounds beautiful!

Gaby: It is. A lot of people say that when they see the Grand Canyon for the first time, it brings tears to their eyes.

Interviewer: Oh! You mean, it makes them cry?

Gaby: Because it's so beautiful, they almost cry, yes.

Interviewer: Did you cry when you first saw the Grand Canyon?

Gaby: Well, I remember thinking like, this is one of the most beautiful things I've ever seen, and I remember feeling very lucky to be seeing it.

Interviewer: Do you know how the Grand Canyon was formed?

Gaby: I think most of it was formed by water. A large river goes through the floor of the Grand Canyon. So basically, I think the river eroded the rock over millions of years and formed the canyon.

Interviewer: So, Jane, tell me about a famous natural landmark in Australia.

Jane: Right. Uluru is a very famous landmark in my country, and one of the most visited sites in Australia.

Interviewer: *Uluru.* That's hard to pronounce! Uluru. Is it a mountain?

Jane: It's a massive, red rock in the center of Australia. I've heard that "Uluru" means "island mountain." It's also called Ayers Rock.

Interviewer: So it used to be a mountain, in the past?

Jane: Yeah. Well, millions of years ago layers of rock were lifted out of the earth. Then over time, the softer rocks eroded away and Uluru is what's left. It's made up of very, very hard minerals. We believe it's more than 300 million years old.

Interviewer: 300 million years old? Incredible!

Jane: Australia is a very special place. We're the oldest continent. We're also the flattest. And Australia is the driest continent where people can live.

Interviewer: I didn't realize that Australia had so many unique features!

Jane: We have a lot of unique and stunning natural places.

Interviewer: Jane, what does Uluru look like?

Jane: It's beautiful! It's a large, red rock in the middle of a very flat area of land. If you look at it from far away, it looks smooth, but if you move closer to the rock, you can see that it has holes in it and is really quite rough.

Interviewer: Really? And what color is it?

Jane: Well, the surface is reddish-brown, but the color can change depending on the time of day. I've seen it look pink, purple, and sometimes gray. When the sun hits it, it looks like it's glowing.

Lecture: Laura Barbieri, "A Look Inside Planet Earth"

Before the Lecture: Listening for main ideas in a lecture, page 11
CD1 TR05

1. Lecture topic.

Today, let's look inside the planet Earth and discuss its internal structure.

2. First main idea.

But first, I want to give you some background information about our planet.

3. Second main idea.

Now, I'd like to discuss each of the three main layers of Earth. First, the crust. …There are two kinds of crust: oceanic and continental.

4. Third main idea.

Moving down from the crust, the next layer of Earth is called the mantle.

5. Fourth main idea.

Finally, continuing downward to the center of the planet, we come to the core. The core can be divided into two parts: an outer core and an inner core.

Lecture Part 1: "Planet Earth: Background"

Listening for supporting details, page 14
CD1 TR06

When you think of the planet Earth, what do you think of? Probably the many natural features that you can see on Earth. For example, you probably think of mountains, forests, deserts, oceans, rivers and lakes, soil and rocks. All of these are important features on the surface of the Earth. But have you ever thought about what's below Earth's surface? Today, let's look inside the planet Earth and discuss its internal structure.

But first, I want to give you some background information about our planet. As you know, there are eight planets in our solar system. Our planet, Earth, is the third planet from the sun. It is also the fifth largest planet in our solar system. How large is Earth? If we draw a line directly through the center of the planet, the distance from the North Pole to the South Pole is almost 13,000 kilometers. Earth is made up of three main layers: the crust, the mantle, and the core. The crust is the outer layer of Earth. The mantle is the next layer, under the crust. The core is the last layer, at the center of Earth. Scientists can study these three layers by using seismic waves. Seismic waves are like waves of energy. Scientists send these waves of energy through the crust, the mantle, and the core, and watch carefully as the waves pass through the three layers. Seismic waves act differently as they pass through different kinds of materials, so scientists can learn important information about Earth's layers.

Lecture Part 2: "Inside Our Planet"

Listening for supporting details, page 16

CD1
TR07 Now, I'd like to discuss each of the three main layers of Earth. First, the crust. Earth's crust is what we see when we look at Earth's surface. If you imagine that Earth is a piece of fruit, the crust is like the skin of the fruit. Our planet's skin is made up of solid rock. There are two kinds of crust: oceanic and continental. Oceanic crust is all of the crust that is covered by Earth's oceans. Actually, most of Earth's crust is oceanic, because most of Earth's surface is covered with water.

Continental crust is the part of the crust that makes up Earth's land areas. Which do you think is thicker: oceanic crust, or continental crust? If you guessed continental crust, you're correct. Oceanic crust is only about 6 to 11 kilometers thick. Continental crust is thicker than oceanic crust, about 30 to 40 kilometers thick. And as I said, both kinds of crust are made up of solid rock.

Moving down from the crust, the next layer of Earth is called the mantle. This layer is much thicker than the crust; the mantle is about 2,900 kilometers deep. The upper part of the mantle is cool, solid rock, like the crust. But the further down you go into the mantle, the more the temperature increases. Because of the higher temperature, the lower part of the mantle is hot and soft.

Finally, continuing downward to the center of the planet, we come to the core. The core can be divided into two parts: an outer core and an inner core. The outer core is very, very hot. It is so hot, in fact, that the rocks here melt and become liquid. Think about that. Deep down below us, near the center of Earth, there is a layer of hot liquid rock!

At the very center of Earth there is a huge ball of very high pressure and high temperature material. This is called the inner core. Scientists believe the inner core is made up of two metals called iron and nickel. The pressure of Earth on this iron and nickel creates a lot of heat. Scientists guess that the temperature of the inner core may be as high as 4,000 degrees Celsius. This heat moves outward from the core and heats the planet from the inside.

Unit 1: Planet Earth
Chapter 2: The Dynamic Earth

CD1
TR08

Getting Started:

Listening for numerical information about distances and rates, page 19

Earth's surface is broken into large pieces called *plates*. These plates are slowly moving all the time. For example, the two large plates under the Atlantic Ocean are moving away from each other. Scientists have measured the rate of movement at about two-and-a-half centimeters per year. In other words, the Atlantic Ocean is slowly growing bigger, by about 2.5 centimeters every year.

The Himalaya Mountains began to form when two plates pushed together 50 million years ago. As the two plates came together, the land was pushed up and formed mountains. Today, the plates are still moving toward each other, and the Himalayas are rising at a rate of about 5 millimeters per year.

Sometimes two plates move past each other side by side. One example of this is in the state of California. The southern part of California is moving northwest, while the northern part of California is moving southeast. The rate of movement is almost 5 centimeters a year. In theory, San Francisco and Los Angeles could move past each other in the future.

The Hawaiian Islands are located in the middle of the Pacific Ocean. The islands are moving in a northwest direction at a rate of about 7 centimeters per year. As they move northwest, they are getting closer and closer to the islands of Japan. In theory, the two groups of islands may meet millions of years in the future.

Interview 1: Living Near an Active Volcano

CD1
TR09 ### Understanding multiple-choice questions, page 22

Interviewer: Loren, you live on the Big Island of Hawaii, one of the most dynamic places on Earth.

Loren: I think the Big Island is *the* most dynamic place on Earth. At least, we have the world's most active volcano.

Interviewer: That sounds interesting! Can you tell me more about your volcano?

Loren: Well, the volcano's name is Kilauea. It is called the world's most active volcano because it has been erupting continuously since 1983. That means it has been erupting for 30 years!

Interviewer: What's it like living near an active volcano?

Loren: It's exciting. I never get tired of watching Kilauea erupt. In the mid '80s, I was working at a school close to the volcano. I will never forget standing on the second floor of the building and seeing a huge fountain of lava shooting up into the air.

Interviewer: You could see a fountain of lava from your school?

Loren: Yes, hot, liquid rock shooting straight up in the air. It was just spectacular. And the sound was so loud. Volcanoes make a very loud sound when they erupt; it was like a plane taking off at an airport. It was awesome!

Interviewer: That does sound awesome.

Loren: And I felt very lucky to see an active volcano since not many people in the world have that opportunity.

Interviewer: And Kilauea is still active today?

Loren: Yes, it is still erupting today. But the lava often flows underground. Sometimes you can see the bright orange lava flowing toward the ocean. When the hot lava meets the ocean it creates a large cloud of steam.

Interviewer: It's probably dangerous, but I would really like to see that.

Loren: [*laughs*] Yeah, when there's an eruption people do want to go see it. But the volcanoes in Hawaii usually do not explode strongly or suddenly. People hurry to see active lava, of course from a distance. It's beautiful.

Interviewer: I guess what they're seeing is new land that is forming on Earth. That lava becomes the newest land on our planet.

Loren: Yes, new land is forming all the time. And scientists are watching Loihi, which is a volcano in the ocean next to the Big Island. Loihi hasn't come to the surface yet. Someday it'll be the newest Hawaiian island.

Interview 2: Living with Earthquakes

CD1 TR10 **Drawing inferences,** page 24

Interviewer: Zack, you grew up in San Francisco, is that right?

Zack: Yes, that's right.

Interviewer: And Yoshiko, you grew up in Tokyo?

Yoshiko: Yes, I'm from Tokyo, Japan.

Interviewer: And now you both live in San Francisco, right?

Zack and Yoshiko: Right.

Interviewer: So you've both had a lot of experiences with earthquakes. Could you tell me about them?

Zack: Well, most earthquakes are very small so usually you don't even know they've happened. Many earthquakes happen when I'm asleep and I don't even notice.

Interviewer: You probably keep sleeping during the small earthquakes.

Zack: Yeah, I just keep sleeping because I don't feel anything. And then there are small ones that happen very quickly and I think, "Oh, was that an earthquake?" It just feels like a little shaking, so I'm not sure if it's an earthquake or not.

Interviewer: Have you ever felt a really strong earthquake?

Zack: The biggest one I've felt, I was at work, in my office. It was a tall building and there was a very strong earthquake. It felt like the floor became liquid, you know, like there was a wave going through the room. And the corners of the office were going up and down like ocean waves.

Interviewer: Yoshiko, have you had similar experiences in Japan?

Yoshiko: Oh yes. I don't remember every earthquake we've had in Japan, but most of the ones I felt were when I was at home.

Interviewer: Oh really?

Yoshiko: Yes, because if you're outside walking or driving, you're not going to notice an earthquake, unless it's a big one. But in my house, everything starts shaking and making noise. I hear the noise first and then I know an earthquake is starting.

Interviewer: Aren't you both afraid when an earthquake happens?

Zack: Like I said, most earthquakes are so small that it's no big deal. I mean no one really notices them or worries about them. When you grow up in an area like San Francisco or Tokyo, areas with a lot of earthquakes, then it's just a part of life. You get training in school, and hopefully you remember what to do if there's real danger.

Interviewer: You get training in school? What kind of training?

Zack: Well, in school, we had earthquake drills. Just like you have fire drills to prepare for a fire. We practice what we would do in case there is a real earthquake. Students get under their desks and the teacher gets in the doorway.

Yoshiko: In Japan, when an earthquake starts, everybody starts opening doors.

Interviewer: I see. Why do you open the doors?

Yoshiko: So later, after the earthquake, we'll be able to go outside. And we know we should go under a desk or table, or in the bathroom. Also, we talk with our family and decide where we should go after an earthquake. Usually it's in the park or the school or some other open space.

Interviewer: So you make an emergency plan.

Zack: Right, because you need to know what to do if you are separated from your family. If you make an emergency plan, you know where to meet your family after the earthquake.

Interviewer: What are other things you do to prepare for an earthquake?

Yoshiko: We try to keep extra water at home.

Zack: Water is the number one thing. And then food is number two. Let's see, what else . . . a flashlight, extra batteries, a radio, extra blankets.

Interviewer: So, living in San Francisco you're not afraid that "the big one" might be coming soon?

Zack: I think earthquakes are amazing — when you imagine how powerful that energy is, powerful enough to shake a huge amount of space and land. But I love San Francisco, and San Francisco has earthquakes, and so it's just part of life. You can't be afraid. I mean, you just have to live your life.

Lecture: Patricia Fryer, "Volcanoes"

Before the Lecture: Focusing on the introduction, page 30

CD1 TR11

Today's lecture is going to be about volcanoes. I love volcanoes! I have loved volcanoes my whole life, ever since I was very young and I saw the volcano Kilauea in Hawaii. I didn't know it then, but I learned later that volcanoes make about 75 percent of all the rocks on the surface of Earth. When you look around and see rocks, remember that most of those rocks — 75% of them — come from volcanoes. So volcanoes are a really important topic when we talk about our natural world.

I'd like to start today's lecture by introducing the basic structure of a volcano — in other words, the different parts that every volcano has. Then I'll describe three basic types of volcanoes: shield volcanoes, composite volcanoes, and super volcanoes. For each basic type, I will also give you an example. Finally, we'll discuss some of the signs that volcanoes exhibit right before they are going to erupt. These are signs in the area around a volcano that scientists can look for that warn that an eruption is about to happen. So let's get started.

Lecture Part 1: "The Basic Structure of a Volcano"

Using telegraphic language, page 32

CD1 TR12

Today's lecture is going to be about volcanoes. I love volcanoes! I have loved volcanoes my whole life, ever since I was very young and I saw the volcano Kilauea in Hawaii. I didn't know it then, but I learned later that volcanoes make about 75 percent of all the rocks on the surface of Earth. When you look around and see rocks, remember that most of those rocks — 75% of them — come from volcanoes. So volcanoes are a really important topic when we talk about our natural world.

I'd like to start today's lecture by introducing the basic structure of a volcano — in other words, the different parts that every volcano has. Then I'll describe three basic types of volcanoes: shield volcanoes, composite volcanoes, and super volcanoes. For each basic type, I will also give you an example. Finally, we'll discuss some of the signs that volcanoes exhibit right before they are going to erupt. These are signs in the area around a volcano that scientists can look for that warn that an eruption is about to happen. So let's get started.

First, the basic structure of a volcano. Well, volcanoes are formed by hot, melted rock called magma. Magma comes from the Earth's mantle, which is a layer deep below Earth's surface. The upper mantle is from 80 to 150 kilometers below Earth's surface, and the temperatures here are so high that rocks start to melt and become magma. This magma flows through the mantle and pushes up against the solid rock above. Usually an eruption starts because an earthquake breaks the rock at the top of the mantle and creates an opening. The magma then rises through the opening in the solid rock and moves towards the surface of the Earth. Finally, the magma comes out of the opening in the crust, called a vent. Now, when magma flows onto the Earth's surface, we don't call it magma anymore. We call it lava. So, melted rock under the Earth's surface is called magma, but melted rock on top of the Earth's surface is called lava.

You probably think of a volcanic eruption as a big, loud explosion, right? But a volcano can erupt gently, as lava that flows along the surface of the Earth. Of course, a volcano can also erupt very powerfully, too. A powerful eruption can have clouds of ash and rock that rise thousands of meters into the sky.

Lecture Part 2: "Types of Volcanoes"

Using telegraphic language, page 35

CD1 TR13

All right, now let's take a look at some of the different types of volcanoes. There are many different types of volcanoes, but today I will tell you about three basic types. The first kind of volcano is what we call a shield volcano. A shield volcano is usually very, very big. Lava flows out from its vent in gentle eruptions. The lava comes out of the vent gently and then flows along the surface of the Earth. The lava cools and becomes hard, forming a broad, circular shape. The shape kind of looks like a shield — broad and circular, with sloping sides — which is why these volcanoes are called "shield" volcanoes. An example of a shield volcano is Mauna Loa in Hawaii. It's the largest volcano on Earth. Mauna Loa starts on the sea floor and rises to over 9,000 meters.

Another type of volcano is the composite volcano. Composite volcanoes are smaller than shield volcanoes. The tallest composite volcanoes are only about 2,500 meters high. Composite volcanoes have both explosive and gentle eruptions. Often, the volcano will start with an explosive eruption and layers of ash and rock will pile up near the vent. Then a gentle eruption happens. The lava flows out and covers the layers of ash from the first eruption, making a cone that has alternating layers of ash and lava. Do you know the meaning of "composite"? It means "made up of different parts." Composite volcanoes get their name because they are made up of different layers of ash and lava. A good example of a composite volcano is Mt. Fuji in Japan. Another example is Mt. St. Helens, which erupted in 1981.

The last type of volcano I'd like to talk about today is a super volcano. Super volcanoes are the biggest volcanoes and have the most explosive eruptions. They don't form a cone shape at all; instead, they leave a huge crater, or hole, in the ground. Eruptions from super volcanoes don't happen very often, but when a super volcano erupts, it causes widespread destruction that affects all life on Earth. Scientists believe that the largest super volcano was Toba. It erupted about 70 to 75 thousand years ago in Indonesia. Some scientists think that the Toba super volcano killed at least 60 percent of all people on Earth.

Pretty scary! But most volcanoes give some signs before they actually erupt, and today scientists are very good at noticing these signs before the eruptions. Some examples of warning signs are earthquakes and ground cracks. Another sign is when drinking water tastes different. Changes in the Earth sometimes affect the way water tastes, so this could be a sign that a volcano will erupt soon. Sometimes ice at the tops of volcanoes starts to melt. Volcanologists who study active volcanoes notice the melting ice and all of the other warning signs and can help in planning for and escaping from dangerous situations.

🔊 Unit 2: Water on Earth
CD1 TR14 Chapter 3: Earth's Water Supply

Getting Started:

Building background vocabulary, page 45

1. [Sound of tide coming in, waves breaking on the shore, with a seagull overhead.]
2. [Sound of heavy rain, with thunder]
3. [Sounds of gentle splashing in water, ducks quacking]
4. [Sound of a geyser shooting steam into the air]
5. [Sound of wind howling, as in a cold, desolate place, sound of ice creaking and then crashing]
6. [Steady, load, roaring sound of a large waterfall]

🔊 Interview 1: Water in the United States
CD1 TR15 Listening for opinions, page 48

Interviewer: So, Gina, we're here to talk about water. Americans are lucky that we don't have to worry about access to water. By that I mean we can get fresh, clean water anytime we want.

Gina: Oh, yeah, I totally agree. I have traveled to places in the world where you can't drink the tap water — in fact, you can't even get tap water on your toothbrush.

Interviewer: Is that because the tap water isn't safe to drink?

Gina: That's right — you always have to boil it, or use water from a bottle. And the first thing I do when I get back to the United States is go pour a glass of water from the tap.

Interviewer: And you really enjoy it?

Gina: Yeah, something like that. It just feels so clean. Like you said, Americans are very lucky, we can just turn on the tap.

Interviewer: Even though we can drink tap water in the United States, there are a lot of people who are worried about our water. For example, some people think that there are pollutants in their drinking water. Is that something you're worried about?

Gina: Well, sure. I mean, just about everywhere you go in this country, there's been some sort of pollution that affects the drinking water. However, I believe that the people who are in charge of the water supply are checking it carefully, and they know if the water is safe to drink.

Interviewer: So, you trust that somebody is checking your water supply and making sure it is clean and safe to drink.

Gina: Yes. I mean, I know that there are some places where it may not be safe. But I feel like I'm lucky because the water where I live seems to be really clean and good to drink.

Interviewer: So you don't drink bottled water or anything like that?

Gina: No, no, I'm happy with our tap water. I buy bottled water sometimes, but mostly for the convenience of having bottles to take in the car. If I buy bottled water, I try to reuse the bottles most of the time.

Interviewer: It's probably a good thing that you don't drink a lot of bottled water, because actually, many people think bottled water hurts the environment.

Gina: Because of its packaging. Right. All those millions of plastic bottles that we drink every day are quickly filling up our landfills. The way I see it, if we could stop using all those plastic bottles, that would help our environment.

🔊 Interview 2: Water in Cambodia
CD1 TR16 Listening for details, page 49

Interviewer: Lara and David, you lived in Cambodia?

Lara: Yeah, we lived in Cambodia for almost four and a half years. Part of the time we were living in Phnom Penh, the capital. It's a very large, growing city. The other part of the time, we lived in the countryside.

Interviewer: I want to talk about the water supply. When you were in Cambodia, did you have any problems getting clean water?

Lara: Well, when we were in Phnom Penh, people would have to buy water from trucks.

Interviewer: So, in the capital city, people didn't have running water in their homes?

David and Lara [simultaneously]: Right. / That's right.

David: When we lived there, many people in the city collected and drank rainwater. Or they bought water and boiled it at home.

Lara: But I think Phnom Penh is better now. The government is trying to provide running water for all the people who live in the city.

Interviewer: Now, you said you also lived in the country. Was access to water better there?

Lara: Umm, no. [laugh]

David: Cambodia has some of the worst problems in the world with water. Thousands of children die from water-borne illnesses every year there.

Interviewer: So, they get sick from drinking the water? And they can die from drinking it?

David: People drink mostly surface water, which means whatever water they can find. In the countryside, people didn't have enough money to buy wood to boil the water, so they would just drink surface water and get sick.

Interviewer: And people get sick because the surface water contains . . . ?

David: Feces.

Lara: Feces of cows, birds, and other animals . . . It all goes into the ponds, where people wash their cows, and then they drink the water.

Interviewer: People don't know that if they drink the water they'll get sick?

David: Well, they know they should boil the water, and sometimes if they have extra wood, they boil it. But they also need the wood to cook their food. So if they can't buy enough wood, they choose to not boil the water.

Interviewer: So, what about you? What did you drink?

David: We tried to bring bottled water with us all the time. If we were out and had to drink their water, we would ask them to boil it first. But it was still not very nice. It was very thick, sort of a tea color, because it's just what you would take out of a river or a pond.

Interview 3: Water in Cameroon

CD1
TR17 **Listening for specific information, page 50**

Interviewer: Seónagh, you lived in Africa. Where did you live, and how long were you there?

Seónagh: I lived in Cameroon, in West Africa. I lived there for just over a year.

Interviewer: Did you have any trouble getting clean, safe water?

Seónagh: Uh-huh, a lot. I was very careful about water because I had been told you could get sick, so I tried to make sure to boil it or buy bottled water.

Interviewer: Did you ever get sick from the water in Cameroon?

Seónagh: No, I never had a problem, so I became more relaxed. I sort of just watched what other people did, and I did what they did. That's what made sense to me, because if they weren't getting sick, then I didn't think that I would get sick.

Interviewer: Mm-hmm, that does make sense.

Seónagh: But I can tell you one story about access to water. You know, some parts of Cameroon have really good roads, and everyone has water.

Interviewer: OK.

Seónagh: But, in this other area that I went to, which is very difficult to get to because the roads are terrible, people would travel, like, sometimes 10 miles to get water. It's just heartbreaking because they had to travel so far just to have water.

Interviewer: Was that because this was a poor area?

Seónagh: Yes. And it's sort of like how people have access to things in the United States. You know, in a poor neighborhood, people do not have the same things as they would in a rich neighborhood.

Interviewer: But water is something that you need to survive. People have to have water every day.

Seónagh: Exactly. In Cameroon, I would see women carrying huge buckets of water on their heads, you know? So what I noticed in Cameroon is that people work very, very hard, and they are able to survive under difficult conditions.

Interviewer: Are people less wasteful of water because of how hard they have to work to get it?

Seónagh: I think people are less wasteful because they have to be. I think that's a natural response to, you know, "This is how much water I have in front of me."

Interviewer: Did living in Cameroon change you and the way you think about water?

Seónagh: Yeah, sure. Because seeing someone walk 10 miles to get a bucket of water, and she has three small children following her . . . it's just heartbreaking.

Interviewer: I'm sure you'll never forget what you saw in Cameroon.

Seónagh: Yeah, and so when I turn on my tap, I'm thinking about the people in Cameroon. That affects how I use water, and how I think of water in the world. You know, water connects all people. The ocean touches every continent, right?

Interviewer: Right.

Seónagh: Water comes from Earth and flows across Earth. It's like blood. In some cultures, water is seen as the blood of Earth. I think of it that way. The Earth is like a living thing. All the plants and animals are parts of the Earth's "body." And everything is connected by water. To me, water is a metaphor for life.

Listening for specific information, page 50

CD1
TR18 **Seónagh:** Water comes from Earth and flows across Earth. It's like blood. In some cultures, water is seen as the blood of Earth. I think of it that way. The Earth is like a living thing. All the plants and animals are parts of the Earth's "body." And everything is connected by water. To me, water is a metaphor for life.

Lecture: Martha McDaniel, "Sources and Functions of Surface Water"

CD1
TR19 **Before the Lecture: Using symbols and abbreviations, page 55**

1. Anyone who has ever been to the ocean, or seen a picture of our planet taken from space, knows that there is plenty of water on Earth. In fact, most of the Earth's surface is covered in water.

2. However, almost all of that water is saltwater. In fact, 97 percent of the water on Earth is saltwater. That means only three percent of the water on Earth is freshwater.

3. Only three percent of the water on Earth is freshwater. But of that three percent, almost 75 percent is in the form of ice in the coldest parts of our planet. That means that only about 25 percent of the freshwater on Earth is in liquid form.

4. This small percentage — less than one percent of all the water on Earth — provides drinking water for every person on Earth, as well as for its plants and animals.

Lecture Part 1: "Sources of Freshwater"

Using symbols and abbreviations, page 57

CD1
TR20 Anyone who has ever been to the ocean, or seen a picture of our planet taken from space, knows that there is plenty of water on Earth. In fact, most of the Earth's surface is covered in water. However, almost all of that water is saltwater. In fact, 97 percent of the water on Earth is saltwater. That means only three percent of the water on Earth is freshwater. That doesn't seem like very much freshwater for people to use and drink, does it? But wait! The amount we can use is even less than that.

As I said, only three percent of the water on Earth is freshwater. But of that three percent, almost 75 percent is in the form of ice in the coldest parts of our planet. That means that only about 25 percent of the freshwater on Earth is in liquid form. This small percentage — less than one percent of all the water on Earth — provides drinking water for every person on Earth, as well as for its plants and animals. Now that's amazing. Today I will talk about this amazing precious resource, Earth's freshwater supply. Where does freshwater come from? When rain or snow falls from the sky, much of the water sinks into the ground and becomes groundwater. But, if the water can't enter the ground, or if the ground is already full of water, then the water stays on the surface. This water starts to move over the surface, and as it flows, it cuts a path into the land. Over time, the path becomes deeper. Now that flow of water is called a stream. Streams are small, but if they combine, or come together, with other streams and become bigger, then we can call it a river. Sometimes, streams and rivers stop flowing and form a pond or lake.

Other times, water keeps flowing across the land until it reaches the ocean.

Of course, freshwater is on the surface of Earth, too. It is in streams, rivers, ponds, and lakes. It helps people in many important ways. Rivers carry nutrients and spread them over the land as they flow. As a result, most land near rivers is rich and fertile, which means it is very good for growing plants. Many farms are located near rivers for this reason. Of course, farmers also need to give their crops freshwater every day to keep them healthy.

People also use freshwater for daily tasks, such as washing dishes and clothes, cleaning and bathing, and so on. Water is used in industry, for transportation, and just for playing and enjoyment. But the most important role of freshwater is to provide clean water for humans and animals to drink. Without freshwater, life on Earth could not exist as it does today.

Lecture Part 2: "Threats to Earth's Freshwater Supply"

CD1
TR21 **Using bullets and brackets to organize your notes, page 59**

As you can see, people, plants, and animals need freshwater to survive. Unfortunately, there are many problems threatening Earth's freshwater supply today. Unsurprisingly, these problems are caused by humans. Land development for human purposes leads to the loss of our natural environment. I'm referring in particular to the construction of buildings, roads, and parking lots. When we cover the earth with concrete, the land can no longer absorb water. In other words, concrete prevents water and nutrients from entering the ground. Land development projects therefore affect Earth's freshwater supply in a negative way.

Pollution also affects our water supply. Pollution comes from many sources: factories, human waste, and fertilizers are just a few examples. Air pollution mixes with the rain, which falls to Earth and then enters the water supply. The trash that people drop on the street may end up in a stream or river. Farmers use fertilizers to help their crops grow, but then these chemicals seep into the ground and into the water. Some water supplies on Earth can no longer be used because they have become so polluted.

However, perhaps the biggest threat to our freshwater supply is overuse by humans. The total amount of water on Earth can never increase. In contrast, the number of people on Earth is increasing all the time. Every year, there are millions of new people on Earth, which means millions more people using and drinking water. An increase in population means a need for more food, which means more farming and more water for crops. People use more water every year, and this is causing problems all over the world. According to the World Water Council, more than

Listening Script **65**

one billion people do not have access to clean, safe water. Water is our most important natural resource. No human could live more than a few days without water. Therefore, we must protect our water supply. People must learn not to waste water. All countries around the world need to cooperate in order to stop pollution and use water more carefully. Only by making changes now can we protect Earth's fresh, clean water for the future.

🔊 Unit 2: Water on Earth
CD1
TR22
Chapter 4: Earth's Oceans

Getting Started:

Expressing likes and dislikes, page 63

1. I'd say swimming is my favorite sport. I really enjoy it. It's great exercise, and I always feel so energized afterwards. As soon as the weather starts to get warm, I look forward to swimming.

2. I'm crazy about fishing. I started fishing when I was in high school, and I've been fishing ever since. I love being near the water under a blue sky, and waiting for a big fish to bite. It's great!

3. My girlfriend loves snorkeling, but I don't really like it myself. The mask and snorkel are uncomfortable to wear. In my opinion, it is hard to breath when I am snorkeling. Honestly, I'd rather go fishing.

4. Windsurfing? Mmm … I don't care for it. Windsurfing is very difficult for me. It looks like a lot of fun, but actually it's hard work. No thank you!

5. Sailing is wonderful! I love it. When the wind is good, you feel like you're flying over the ocean in a sailboat.

🔊 Interview 1: Adventure Under the Ocean
CD1
TR23
Retelling what you have heard, page 66

Interviewer: I know you love to dive, Edmund. How did you first get interested in diving?

Edmund: Well, when I was younger, I wanted to be a marine biologist. I really wanted to study the ocean, and learn all about life in the ocean. So, I thought, "Maybe I should learn how to dive."

Interviewer: So did you take a diving class?

Edmund: First I had to learn how to swim, because I wasn't a good swimmer. So, I took a swimming class. Then when I was in high school, I got certified in scuba diving. I started diving then, and I've never stopped.

Interviewer: When you dive with your equipment, your tank, how long can you stay underwater?

Edmund: Let's see…the longest I've stayed down is a little over three hours. But usually I'm down for just 45 minutes or so.

Interviewer: And why do you dive? Is it just for fun?

Edmund: Yeah, for fun. I do it to relax, to see things. And I often see something or find something interesting.

Interviewer: Like what?

Edmund: OK, like the last thing I found were these really old bottles. Like I found one bottle from the early 1900s. I was really surprised when I saw the date. I found some other bottles too, but that one was the oldest.

Interviewer: 100 years old — that is surprising!

Edmund: And then a few months ago, maybe, I was out diving and a sea horse swam by. It's unusual to see that kind of fish, so I took a picture.

Interviewer: So you take photographs underwater, too.

Edmund: Yes, I always carry my camera. I like to show other people that I saw something. Because if I tell people, "I saw a sea horse," they go, "Yeah, right."

Interviewer: What is it about diving that you like so much? I mean, why haven't you gotten bored with it after all these years?

Edmund: Well, I think it's an adventure. It adds a lot to my life. I have all of these experiences, interesting experiences that a lot of people don't have. Diving never feels boring to me.

Interviewer: And you said you do it to relax?

Edmund: Yeah. To me, it's very peaceful. The ocean is very quiet and calm … you can just sit there and look at the fish. It's very relaxing.

Interviewer: So the ocean never feels threatening to you at all? Don't you sometimes feel scared?

Edmund: No. Well, when I first started diving by myself, I used to always turn around to look for the shark that would come and get me. [*laughs*] It never was there. So I guess you stop worrying about it. Although there were a couple times when I felt scared. …

Interviewer: For example?

Edmund: Well . . . a few times an eel has hit me while I was diving. The first time, I felt something hit my hand, and I looked down and saw something gray swimming around my chest. And then it swam away.

Interviewer: Wow.

Edmund: And another time, I was swimming along, and I looked up and saw two huge fins, and I started panicking because the fins were bigger than me. So, I was like [*breathing fast and hard*] and then I told myself, "OK, those are whales, calm down."

Interviewer: You swam into a whale??

Edmund: I was swimming along next to one. And then I guess the whale heard me, because it just starting slowly rising up and went to the surface. When it did that, I could see that there was another whale, a baby.

Interviewer: Swimming with whales! Now that's a very special experience.

Edmund: I went to the surface to look for them but they swam away.

Interviewer: When you're down there, diving and swimming under the water, do you feel like you're part of the ocean environment?

Edmund: I feel like a visitor, you know. Especially when the ocean pushes you around. Sometimes I can't get to where I want to go, so I have to go someplace else to look around.

Interviewer: You mean you can't always control where you want to go, and you have to follow the ocean.

Edmund: Yes, exactly.

Interview 2: Surf's Up
CD1
TR24 **Listening for main ideas,** page 67

Interviewer: Hey Tomoki, let's start with some background questions. When did you first begin surfing and why?

Tomoki: Hmm, I started surfing . . . I believe about five years ago. I'd always been interested in the sport, and I finally started when one of my friends gave me a surfboard. Since I had my own surfboard, I just thought I'd give it a shot.

Interviewer: Did you love surfing right away?

Tomoki: Yeah, right away. Part of the reason is, I've always loved the ocean. When I was a child, I remember that every summer I spent all my time at the beach, playing in the water. So, yeah, when I tried surfing, I couldn't even sit or stand up on the board, but I still liked it.

Interviewer: I've heard that it's pretty hard to stand up on a surfboard. Most people can't do it the first time they go surfing. Is that true?

Tomoki: It's challenging. It's not something you can do right away. You need to practice. Surfing is just like any other sport — you need to practice to be good at it.

Interviewer: Other than practice, what else do you need to be a good surfer?

Tomoki: Well, I think physically, you need to be fit. That means your body has to be strong so that you can swim. And in order to stand up on the board, you need to have good balance. That's the physical part.

Interviewer: Is there anything else you need for good surfing?

Tomoki: Well, you need to have waves. [laughs]

Interviewer: Obviously! And what about wind? Is wind good for surfing or not?

Tomoki: Not too good. Usually surfers hope that there's no wind.

Interviewer: But doesn't the wind bring the waves?

Tomoki: Yeah, but if there's too much wind, the surface of the ocean is not that clean. We say that the surface is choppy or clean. Surfers always want to have a clean surface.

Interviewer: Now, could you describe to a non-surfer what it feels like to surf?

Tomoki: Well, it feels like you're sliding over the wave, but the wave is always moving. It's very dynamic, because everything is moving together.

Interviewer: OK, I can imagine that.

Tomoki: It feels like you're flying through the water. And the shape of the wave is so beautiful. Sometimes, you can see inside the ocean — you can actually look inside the wave and see fish and the ocean floor. How does it feel? It just feels good.

Interviewer: Do you feel that you're controlling your surfboard, or do you have to go where the wave takes you?

Tomoki: Hmm… both. You really feel the power of nature, the power of the waves in your whole body. The waves are moving your entire body through the ocean.

Interviewer: That's a lot of power!

Tomoki: And you need that power. But, you also need to be able to control the movement of your board. There's nothing else like it. That's why I love surfing — it's unique.

Thinking critically about the topic, page 67
CD1
TR25 **Listen to the last part of the interview with Edmund.**

Interviewer: When you're down there, diving and swimming under the water, do you feel like you're part of the ocean environment?

Edmund: I feel like a visitor, you know. Especially when the ocean pushes you around. Sometimes I can't get to where I want to go, so I have to go someplace else to look around.

Interviewer: You mean you can't always control where you want to go, and you have to follow the ocean.

Edmund: Yes, exactly.

Now listen to the last part of the interview with Tomoki.

Interviewer: Do you feel that you're controlling your surfboard, or do you have to go where the wave takes you?

Tomoki: Hmm… both. You really feel the power of nature, the power of the waves in your whole body. The waves are moving your entire body through the ocean.

Interviewer: That's a lot of power!

Tomoki: And you need that power. But, you also need to be able to control the movement of your board. There's nothing else like it. That's why I love surfing — it's unique.

Lecture: Glen Jackson, "One World Ocean"

Before the Lecture: Listening for signal words and
CD1
TR26 **phrases,** page 72

1. Some people say that there is one more ocean, called the Southern Ocean, down near the Antarctic continent. However, not all scientists agree that the Southern Ocean is a separate ocean basin.

2. The sun heats the seawater in this upper layer. Therefore, the surface layer is sometimes called the "sunlit zone."

3. The biggest difference between the surface layer and the middle layer is the temperature of the water. As I just said, the surface layer is relatively warm, with an average temperature of 17 degrees Celsius.

4. Sunlight becomes much weaker below the sunlit zone, so no plants can grow in the middle layer. Consequently, most of the animals living in this layer have to swim up to the surface layer to find food.

5. The animals that live here have to adapt to be able to live in this cold and dark environment. For example, many fish in the midnight zone do not have eyes.

Lecture Part 1: "The World's Oceans"

Using handouts to help you take notes, page 74

CD1
TR27 The topic of our lecture today is Earth's oceans. The percentage of our planet that is covered by ocean water is actually very high. The planet is divided into two halves: the northern hemisphere, which is the top half of the Earth, and the southern hemisphere, or the bottom half. Eighty percent of the southern hemisphere is ocean. As for the top half, 61 percent of the northern hemisphere is ocean. Less than the southern hemisphere, but still quite a bit. The result is that 71 percent of the planet's surface is ocean and only 29 percent is land. Naturally all of the oceans are connected, so we can think of it as one world ocean, which is divided into four main ocean basins. These four basins are the Atlantic, the Pacific, the Indian, and the Arctic.

First we have the Atlantic Ocean, which stretches between Europe and Africa and the Americas. Next, the Pacific Ocean, which is the largest and deepest ocean. The Pacific stretches between the Americas and Asia. Moving south, we have the Indian Ocean, which is easy to remember because it surrounds the country of India. And then, in the northern regions of our planet, we also have the Arctic Ocean, which is the smallest and shallowest ocean. Some people say that there is one more ocean, called the Southern Ocean, down near the Antarctic continent. However, not all scientists agree that the Southern Ocean is a separate ocean basin.

Again, the oceans are not actually separated. They are all connected, and water is constantly mixing and moving from one ocean to the other. This is why we can think of all our planet's oceans as one world ocean.

Earth's oceans are very, very deep. The average depth from the surface of the ocean down to the ocean floor is 4,200 meters. As one goes down from the surface, one finds a very interesting feature: the ocean has a layered structure. This is because seawater has different densities. Density has to do with "heaviness" — the quantity of

matter in a particular space or area. In the next part of our lecture, I'd like to look in more detail at the ocean's layered structure.

Lecture Part 2: "The Layers of the Ocean"

Using handouts to help you take notes, page 76

CD1
TR28 An interesting feature of the ocean is its layered structure. Let's talk about each of the three main layers, one by one. The first layer is called the surface layer. The surface layer is the top 100 to 200 meters of the ocean. The sun heats the seawater in this upper layer. Therefore, the surface layer is sometimes called the "sunlit zone." Its warmth and light permeate the surface layer, making it an ideal place for many forms of life. Most of the ocean's fish and other marine life are near the surface layer, where they can find a lot of algae and other plants to eat.

Beneath the first 200 meters or so of the ocean, the surface layer ends and the middle layer begins. The middle ocean layer goes down to about 1,000 meters in depth. The biggest difference between the surface layer and the middle layer is the temperature of the water. As I just said, the surface layer is relatively warm, with an average temperature of 17 degrees Celsius. By contrast, in the middle layer, the temperature drops very quickly. With every meter you go down, the temperature becomes colder and colder. By 1,000 meters, the average temperature of the ocean water is only 4 degrees Celsius. Sunlight becomes much weaker below the sunlit zone, so no plants can grow in the middle layer. Consequently, most of the animals living in this layer have to swim up to the surface layer to find food.

Below the middle layer of the ocean, there is the bottom layer, which is all the cold, dense water below 1,000 meters in depth. As you can imagine, there is no sunlight here at all, so the water is pitch black. As a result, this layer is sometimes called the "midnight zone." It has very cold, almost freezing temperatures. The animals that live here have to adapt to be able to live in this cold and dark environment. For example, many fish in the midnight zone do not have eyes. Some animals here make and give off their own light. Much of the ocean's bottom layer hasn't been studied yet, so scientists still don't know a lot about this deep environment.

So let's just review very quickly what we talked about today. We have four main oceans: the Atlantic, the Pacific, the Indian Ocean, and the Arctic Ocean. All of the oceans are connected, and as a result we can describe them as one world ocean. The oceans are deep and have a layered structure: there's a surface layer, a middle layer, and a bottom layer. There's much, much more to say about the ocean. It's the last unexplored region on Earth.

Focusing on the conclusion, page 77

 CD1 TR29 So let's just review very quickly what we talked about today. We have four main oceans: the Atlantic, the Pacific, the Indian Ocean, and the Arctic Ocean. All of the oceans are connected, and as a result we can describe them as one world ocean. The oceans are deep and have a layered structure: there's a surface layer, a middle layer, and a bottom layer. There's much, much more to say about the ocean. It's the last unexplored region on Earth.

Unit 3: The Air Around Us
CD2 TR01
Chapter 5: Earth's Atmosphere

Getting Started:

Listening for background noise, page 87

Listen. Where is the person in picture A?

[sounds of a rain forest; a man sounding as though he is hot and uncomfortable]

Listen. Where is the person in picture B?

[sounds of the countryside; a woman sneezing]

Listen. Where is the person in picture C?

[sounds of a strong wind, whistling, howling; a man who is having trouble breathing as he hikes up a mountain]

Listen. Where is the person in picture D?

[city sounds; a man coughing]

 CD2 TR02 **Listening for background noise,** page 87

Listen. Why is the person in each picture having problems?

Picture A. [Same sounds as previous track] It's so hot here. And humid, too. I'm going to need to take a shower because I'm sweating so much.

Picture B. [Same sounds as previous track] I should have stayed at home today. There is so much pollen in the air. And my allergies are so bad — I can't stop sneezing!

Picture C. [Same sounds as previous track] Oh, it's difficult to breathe up here. The air is so thin. I can't get enough oxygen into my lungs.

Picture D. [Same sounds as previous track] Oh, boy the traffic's bad today. The air feels really dirty. Oh, I hope I don't get sick.

 CD2 TR03 **Interview 1: Pollutants in the Air**

Listening for specific information, page 90

Interviewer: Jeff, you work for an environmental organization, is that right?

Jeff: Yes, that's right. I'm the director of an organization that tries to protect our natural environment in many different ways.

Interviewer: And one of the ways your group helps the environment is by protecting air quality?

Jeff: Right. We're always thinking about air quality and its effects on people and nature.

Interviewer: What are some factors that affect air quality?

Jeff: Ah, well, there are a number of factors that affect air quality. First, there are a lot of pollutants in the air. …

 CD2 TR04 **Interview 1: Pollutants in the Air**

Listening for specific information, page 90

Interviewer: Jeff, you work for an environmental organization, is that right?

Jeff: Yes, that's right. I'm the director of an organization that tries to protect our natural environment in many different ways.

Interviewer: And one of the ways your group helps the environment is by protecting air quality?

Jeff: Right. We're always thinking about air quality and its effects on people and nature.

Interviewer: What are some factors that affect air quality?

Jeff: Ah, well, there are a number of factors that affect air quality. First, there are a lot of pollutants in the air, and many of these pollutants come from human activities, meaning things that people are doing or making.

Interviewer: Can you give some examples of pollutants made by humans?

Jeff: Well, the most common human-made pollutants that you see come from burning fuels. For example, when factories burn oil, natural gas, or coal, this creates pollutants that go into the air.

Interviewer: And cars, right? I think that's the example that most people think of.

Jeff: Cars create a number of pollutants in the air. Have you ever heard of particulate matter? Particulate matter is tiny pieces of matter that are small enough to float in the air. Cars make a lot of particulate matter.

Interviewer: Can you see particulate matter in the air?

Jeff: Well, you can when there's enough of it. In fact, if you look at a factory, sometimes you can see a dark cloud coming out of it.

Interviewer: Oh, I know what you mean — that big cloud of smoke that comes out of the top of the building.

Jeff: That's the particulate matter. Some of it falls on the ground; you know, if you're in an area with many factories, you might see a black or gray coating on cars or on the ground. That's the particulate matter.

Interviewer: That's terrible!

Jeff: But some particulate matter is so small, very small particles, you can't see it at all.

Interviewer: So people don't notice when they breathe it in?

Jeff: Usually not. But even though we can't feel it, it can cause damage to our lungs.

Interviewer: We've talked a lot about particulate matter that is made by humans. Are there any natural sources of particulate matter?

Jeff: Natural sources…well, one is wildfire that starts naturally from lightning or something like that. When a wildfire burns, it sends a lot of particulate matter into the air. Similarly, a windstorm, like in the desert, blows pieces of soil into the air. So wildfire, windstorms, these are a couple of examples of natural sources.

Interview 2: Air Quality
CD2
TR05 **Listening for specific information, page 91**

Interviewer: Shari, you live in a big city. Tell me about the air quality there.

Shari: Well, it can be bad, especially in the summertime. There are mountains near my home, but you can't even see the mountains at certain times of the year because the air is so bad.

Interviewer: By "bad" you mean … polluted? dirty?

Shari: Dirty *and* polluted!

Interviewer: What does it actually look like, when the air quality is bad?

Shari: It looks hazy . . . it's like fog, but it's brown like smoke, and that's why they call it "smog." Smog comes from the words "smoke" and "fog" mixed together; you get "smog." So, anyway, the air just looks hazy, but it's brown.

Interviewer: When the air quality is bad, does it affect you physically?

Shari: Sure. When there is a lot of smog, I get really bad headaches. Sometimes my headaches are so bad, I can hardly think. And it is difficult to breathe.

Interviewer: That sounds dangerous!

Shari: During the weather report, they always include a smog level advisory. It's basically a system to tell people if the air quality is good or bad. I think it's between zero and five, where five is dangerous and zero is completely clear. Any time it's over three or four, they warn people to be careful.

Interviewer: So this advisory tells you how much smog is in the air.

Shari: Right, the amount of pollution. When I was in school, whenever the advisory was above three or four, when we went to PE we weren't allowed to exercise outside.

Interviewer: It's not safe to be outside?

Shari: Uh-uh. When it reaches a certain level, the city decides that it's dangerous to exercise outdoors, so they tell people to stay indoors at these times.

Listening for specific information, page 91
CD2
TR06 **Shari:** It looks hazy . . . it's like fog, but it's brown like smoke, and that's why they call it "smog." Smog comes from the words "smoke" and "fog" mixed together; you get "smog." So, anyway, the air just looks hazy, but it's brown.

Interviewer: When the air quality is bad, does it affect you physically?

Shari: Sure. When there is a lot of smog, I get really bad headaches. Sometimes my headaches are so bad, I can hardly think. And it is difficult to breathe.

Interviewer: That sounds dangerous!

Shari: During the weather report, they always include a smog level advisory. It's basically a system to tell people if the air quality is good or bad. I think it's between zero and five, where five is dangerous and zero is completely clear. Any time it's over three or four, they warn people to be careful.

Interviewer: So this advisory tells you how much smog is in the air.

Shari: Right, the amount of pollution. When I was in school, whenever the advisory was above three or four, when we went to PE we weren't allowed to exercise outside.

Interviewer: It's not safe to be outside?

Shari: Uh-uh. When it reaches a certain level the city decides that it's dangerous to exercise outdoors, so they tell people to stay indoors at these times.

Interview 3: Humid and Dry Air
CD2
TR07 **Answering multiple-choice questions, page 93**

Interviewer: Kelley and Michael, thank you for talking to us about air today. Kelley, you live in a humid environment, and Michael, you lived in a very dry environment.

[Speaking at the same time] **Kelley:** Yup. **Michael:** Yes, I did.

Interviewer: Kelley, I know that you're a very athletic person. What sports do you like?

Kelley: Well, I like hiking, running, volleyball . . . I also like basketball, and I especially love cycling.

Interviewer: Could you tell me how the air affects you as an athlete?

Kelley: I think the most important factor for athletes is humidity.

Interviewer: The amount of water in the air?

Kelly: Exactly. So if it's humid, if there's more water in the air, it can be very uncomfortable for athletes.

Interviewer: Why is that?

Kelley: Because when you're playing sports, your body makes a lot of heat. You need to get rid of some of that heat by sweating.

Interviewer: I see. Sweating is important because it takes the heat out of our bodies. But how is that related to humidity?

Kelley: Well, if it's humid, there's already a lot of water in the air, so the sweat stays on your skin and you still feel hot. But if the air is dry, the sweat can evaporate and cool your skin.

Interviewer: So when it's humid, it's harder to cool your body down?

Kelley: Right. And you may feel more tired.

Interviewer: Michael, humidity was not a problem for you, right?

Michael: Not at all. I lived in a very dry place.

Interviewer: Did you live in the desert?

Michael: Yes, for a short time I was living in the desert near Mexico. They only get two to three inches of rain in a year, so it's very, very dry.

Interviewer: And hot?

Michael: Yep, it's one of the hottest places in the world, actually. One day, I remember, it was very hot and dry, and the wind blew up a dust storm.

Interviewer: What was that like?

Michael: Well, it was like fog. I couldn't really see anything. I was driving with my friends, and we stopped our car.

Interviewer: Did you get out of your car?

Michael: Just for a minute. The wind was blowing the sand all around us, just like in the movies. And it was so hot! We spent maybe one minute outside the car, and then we said, "This is crazy, let's get out of here!"

Interviewer: Did living in the desert affect you physically?

Michael: It was difficult to get used to the strong heat. I had to drink a lot more than usual to make sure my body got enough water. In fact I probably drank, oh, a half-gallon to a gallon of sports drinks a day.

Interviewer: How was the air quality?

Michael: Most of the time, the air was very clean. But it did dry you out. I noticed that my lips and skin were dry all the time.

Interviewer: Was it hard to breathe the air?

Michael: Oh yes! When it was really hot and dry, you had to be careful not to exercise too much. It would almost hurt your lungs. You'd want to wait until it cooled down a bit in the evening.

  **Lecture: Ken Needham, "What Is in the Air Out There?"**

CD2 TR08 **Before the Lecture: Identifying key vocabulary in the lecture, page 97**

1. The amount of water vapor in the air — in other words, the humidity level — is something I know you're all familiar with.

2. Have you ever thought about the idea of solids in the air? The term *particulate matter* is defined as any tiny pieces of solids that are small enough to float in the air.

3. Flowers, trees, plants — they release pollen, or a powder made by flowers, and other natural matter.

4. Humans also add particulate matter to the air. Because of human actions, there are some substances in the air that shouldn't be there, or there's too much of certain substances, and this is what we know as pollution.

 Lecture Part 1: "Humidity"

CD2 TR09 **Organizing your notes in an outline, page 99**

Take a deep breath [lecturer inhales and exhales audibly]. Have you ever thought about what you breathe in, every time you take a breath? We can't see it, we can't feel it, but air is all around us. Because we can't see air, we often think that air is empty. But air actually contains many different things. So today I'd like to talk about what's in the air out there.

You probably know that air around you is composed of a lot of different gases. The two main gases that make up the air are nitrogen and oxygen. Nitrogen makes up 78 percent and oxygen makes up 21 percent of the air we breathe. But there are also about 10 other gases that are in the air, in very small amounts. And even though we can't see or smell or taste these gases, we could not live without them.

The amount of water vapor in the air — in other words, the humidity level — is something I know you're all familiar with. If you hear on the news that today's humidity is 80 or 90 percent, that means there's a lot of water vapor in the air. If you are outdoors and it is hot and humid, your clothes will probably feel sticky and you'll probably feel uncomfortable. But if you hear that today's humidity is 50 percent, that means there's a lot less water in the air. Fifty percent is comfortable for most people. Deserts and other dry places can have a humidity level of only 10 percent — not much water in the air at all. When you're outside in 10 percent humidity, your mouth will probably feel dry and you'll need to drink something soon.

Before we move on, let's talk about how water vapor gets into the air. The most obvious source is rain, snow, and other forms of liquid or solid water that falls from the clouds. Sometimes the rain or snow changes to vapor as it falls, and it stays in the air. But water vapor can also enter the air from sources on Earth: from oceans and rivers, from trees, plants, and even from the ground.

Lecture Part 2: "Particulate Matter"

CD2 TR10 **Organizing your notes in a chart, page 101**

So far we've talked about gases and water vapor in the air. Have you ever thought about the idea of solids in the air?

The term *particulate matter* is defined as any tiny pieces of solids that are small enough to float in the air. Now, these tiny pieces of matter are so small that they're carried in the air, and they're too light to fall to the ground. There are many different kinds of particulate matter; some are found in the air naturally, and others are human-made, that is, they're the result of human activity. I'd like to talk about a couple of different types of particulate matter. Let's start with particulate matter that occurs naturally. When a volcano erupts, it shoots smoke and ash into the air. In the same way, a forest fire fills the air up with smoke. When the ocean waves crash against the shore, salt and sand fly into the air. Flowers, trees, plants — they release pollen, or a powder made by flowers, and other natural matter. Have you ever walked through a field and then started sneezing? That might be pollen in the air entering your nose. Dirt and dust from the environment may be picked up by the wind, then fly into our eyes and make them red and itchy. All of these are examples of naturally occurring particulate matter that is found in the air.

Humans also add particulate matter to the air. Because of human actions, there are some substances in the air that shouldn't be there, or there's too much of certain substances, and this is what we know as pollution. When humans burn wood for cooking and heating, or they burn plants or trees, they add particulate matter to the air. When humans cut down trees and take water from the land, it's easier for dirt and dust to be picked up and carried in the air. But the activity that creates the most pollution is the burning of coal and other fossil fuels. This means every time we use fuel to power a factory or run a car, pollution is added to the air we breathe.

When we breathe these particles in, they can hurt our eyes, our throats, and our noses, or cause more serious health problems. Let me just remind you, the next time you look around at all that "empty" air, there really is a lot out there.

Unit 3: The Air Around Us
CD2
TR11 **Chapter 6: Weather and Climate**

Getting Started:
Listening for specific information, page 104

1. It's going to be a beautiful day today! We're looking at a clear sky, no clouds, and warm temperatures. Be sure to get outside and enjoy the weather!

2. You may want to leave work early this afternoon, everyone. It's already very cloudy out there, and we have some strong wind. The thunderstorm will be here in about an hour. Be careful driving!

3. It's getting colder and colder. It has been raining all morning, but soon that rain will change to snow. It

looks like temperatures are going to get even colder tonight, so be prepared for a lot of snow tomorrow morning.

4. The good news is, the heavy rain has ended. The bad news is, we're still going to have a lot of fog today. But it's definitely better than yesterday.

Interview 1: A Future Meteorologist
CD2
TR12 **Listening for specific information, page 106**

Interviewer: Sara, tell me a little bit about yourself.

Sara: OK, I'm from Portugal, and right now I'm a graduate student. I'm studying meteorology.

Interviewer: Could you explain what meteorology is?

Sara: Well, meteorology is the study of our planet's atmosphere. It is a way of describing and trying to understand what happens in the atmosphere.

Interviewer: How did you become interested in meteorology?

Sara: It's funny, when I was a teenager, I couldn't decide what I wanted to be. My father always told me science is a good subject to study. He said, "Science is very good, scientists can do many things." I guess he influenced me, because I chose science as my major.

Interviewer: So your father influenced your decision to study meteorology.

Sara: Yes. And another reason is, I've always had a fascination with the sky. When I was young, I would stare at the sky, looking at the clouds and watching them pass.

Interviewer: You liked to watch the clouds!

Sara: I wanted to know why one cloud is different from another one. And one day when I was around 17 years old, I told my mother, "Why don't I study meteorology? I like the sky!"

Interviewer: Are you happy that you chose meteorology as your major?

Sara: Yes, very happy. Our atmosphere is so important. People don't realize . . . I think because we can't see air, we think the air is nothing. But that's not true.

Interviewer: Of course not! We all need air to survive.

Sara: Think of it this way: Earth is like a big aquarium, we're just like fish who live in the aquarium, and our atmosphere is just like water. Fish need water to survive, and we need air. Without the atmosphere, all human beings on Earth would die.

Listening for specific information, page 106
CD2
TR13 **Sara:** Our atmosphere is so important. People don't realize . . . I think because we can't see air, we think the air is nothing. But that's not true.

Interviewer: Of course not! We all need air to survive.

Sara: Think of it this way: Earth is like a big aquarium, we're just like fish who live in the aquarium, and our atmosphere is just like water. Fish need water to survive, and we need air. Without the atmosphere, all human beings on Earth would die.

Interview 2: Severe Weather

CD2 TR14 **Predicting the content,** page 107

1. Interviewer: Dorothy, tell us about your experience.
Dorothy: Well, I was in a blizzard last October. It really was a freak storm. I mean, generally we don't get much snow in New York in October, but this was *a lot* of snow.
2. Interviewer: Yukiya, what kind of severe weather did you experience?
Yukiya: In my case, I was caught in a flood about two years ago.
3. Interviewer: Evylynn, you were also in a dangerous situation.
Evylynn: That's right. When I was 16 years old, a hurricane struck my hometown.

Interview 2: Severe Weather

CD2 TR15 **Predicting the content,** page 108

Interviewer: You've all had experiences with severe weather. Dorothy, tell us about your experience.
Dorothy: Well, I was in a blizzard last October. It really was a freak storm. I mean, generally we don't get much snow in New York in October, but this was *a lot* of snow.
Interviewer: Did the snow come quickly?
Dorothy: Yes, very quickly. The snow started falling on a Thursday, and it was falling very fast, and by Friday morning we had about two feet of it.
Interviewer: Two feet of snow!
Dorothy: The worst part was that it was very heavy, wet snow. And the weight of the snow brought down a lot of tree branches. And then, when the tree branches broke, they fell onto the power lines, and the power lines came down, too.
Interviewer: Oh no! That means no electricity.
Dorothy: Right. After the blizzard, so many people were left without electricity. The power was off for two weeks, in some places even longer.
Interviewer: How about you — did you lose power in your home?
Dorothy: Yes, but we were lucky. Our power came back on after four days.
Interviewer: Yukiya, what kind of severe weather did you experience?
Yukiya: In my case, I was caught in a flood about two years ago.
Interviewer: A flood! So … you were caught in a lot of water?
Yukiya: Mm-hmm. A lot of water, caused by a lot of rain!

Interviewer: What do you remember about it?
Yukiya: I remember I was at school, studying, and at that time I was stressed out about my homework, you know? And it was raining really hard, but I didn't pay much attention to it. Then all of a sudden the lights went out.
Interviewer: You lost power?
Yukiya: Yeah, no power. So I went outside, and when I opened the door, I saw all this water pouring into the parking lot!
Interviewer: Coming toward you?
Yukiya: Well, it was flooding into the parking lot. It looked like a big pool. But I had to get out of there, so I had to go through the water. First, it came up to my knees, and then it came up to my waist. I actually saw one car floating!
Interviewer: Was it still raining?
Yukiya: It was raining really hard. And all around me there was water and mud and tree branches, and all kinds of broken things. It was crazy.
Interviewer: Were you scared?
Yukiya: Yes, I was scared, but at the same time, I was kind of excited. I'd never seen anything like that before. I was like, "This is definitely going to be on the news!"
Interviewer: Did you get out of the flood safely?
Yukiya: Yes, I finally got out, and I went home. I was fine, just, you know . . . I was soaking wet!
Interviewer: Evylynn, you were also in a dangerous situation.
Evylynn: That's right. When I was 16 years old, a hurricane struck my hometown.
Interviewer: And this was a very powerful hurricane?
Evylynn: It was a Category 4 hurricane, so one of the strongest hurricanes to ever hit the United States.
Interviewer: Do you remember what it was like when the hurricane hit your hometown?
Evylynn: I remember when the hurricane hit, it was amazing. Houses right across the street from me were torn apart. Trees were pulled out of the ground and thrown down the street.
Interviewer: Wow! The wind was pulling the trees out of the ground?
Evylynn: Yeah, trees and lampposts were flying everywhere.
Interviewer: Scary.
Evylynn: Yes, it was scary, but I also thought it was kind of fun. I guess that sounds strange, but I was pretty young at the time, so it was exciting. Of course I was worried about the families in the houses that were destroyed.
Interviewer: Was your house damaged?
Evylynn: No, my house wasn't damaged badly. We were lucky. But after the hurricane, the whole town didn't have power for a couple of months.

Interviewer: What a terrible experience.

Evylynn: But you know, I learned a lot from that experience. Now I know if there's ever a warning about a natural disaster, I need to take it seriously. Once you experience something like that, you remember it for the rest of your life.

Listening for opinions, page 108

CD2 TR16 **Interviewer:** I'd like to ask you about global warming. Sara, you're a meteorology student. Do you think global warming is affecting our weather on Earth?

Sara: Well, my opinion is, global warming is really happening, and everybody knows that. And everybody knows that human beings are a little bit responsible for it. But as for the weather, there are some changes that I think are natural . . . changes that would probably happen even without people. . . .

Interviewer: So, in your opinion, global warming is *not* affecting our weather?

Sara: I don't know. With science, until you have the right answer, you can't say for sure. I can't say for sure if global warming is affecting our weather or not.

Interviewer: Dorothy, do you think global warming is affecting our weather?

Dorothy: Personally, I do. Just look at the weather these days. Hurricanes are becoming stronger and more severe. I don't think it's just the natural cycle of things.

Interviewer: And you think the cause is global warming?

Dorothy: Yes. I can see how the weather has changed just in my hometown. The winters used to be longer and colder, and now they're warmer and there isn't as much snow.

Interviewer: Yukiya?

Yukiya: I agree with Dorothy. I'm not a scientist or anything, but I've heard that global warming is melting the ice in Antarctica, and the water level of our oceans is going up, and that's what causes the hurricanes. I'm sure global warming is having some effect on the weather.

Interviewer: Evylynn?

Evylynn: I agree. I think global warming is making the weather worse, and there's more risk of dangerous weather. Because humans are changing Earth, that's causing the weather to change. We need to start doing something soon to protect our environment, or it's all going to be gone.

Lecture: Fred Mackenzie, "Global Warming"

Before the Lecture: Listening for numerical
CD2 TR17 information, page 112

1. Since the beginning of Earth, about 4.6 billion years ago, there has been a mixture of gases surrounding the planet.

2. The atmosphere acts as a kind of a shield and a filter. It reflects about thirty percent of the sun's energy back into space. About 70 percent of it actually passes through the atmosphere. Of that 70 percent, much of it is absorbed by the clouds and air. Only half of the energy that passes through the atmosphere — about 35 percent — reaches the Earth's surface, which is warmed by the sun's energy.

3. This has led to a heating of Earth's surface. In the past 100 years, scientists have found an increase of one degree centigrade in the average temperature on Earth.

4. But unless we change the way we do things today — which means we must stop relying on fossil fuels for 80 percent of our energy supply — the amount of greenhouse gases will continue to increase, and temperatures will continue to go up.

Lecture Part 1: "The Greenhouse Effect"

 Copying a lecturer's illustrations, page 113

CD2 TR18 Well, the topic of my lecture today is global warming, but before I talk about that, I'm going to give you some background information about Earth's atmosphere. As you already know, the atmosphere is what we call the layer of gases that surrounds the planet. Since the beginning of Earth, about 4.6 billion years ago, there has been a mixture of gases surrounding the planet. Some of these gases are called "greenhouse gases." We call them greenhouse gases because they create a "greenhouse effect." That is, they make the atmosphere warmer, because they absorb heat from the sun.

Let's look more closely at the interactions that lead to the greenhouse effect. Energy from the sun is the force behind our climate systems. It approaches Earth and enters the outer layers of our atmosphere. The atmosphere acts as a kind of a shield and a filter. It reflects about thirty percent of the sun's energy back into space. About 70 percent of it actually passes through the atmosphere. Of that 70 percent, much of it is absorbed by the clouds and air. Only half of the energy that passes through the atmosphere — about 35 percent — reaches the Earth's surface, which is warmed by the sun's energy. The Earth emits, or sends, this energy back towards the atmosphere. About ten percent of it leaks back into space, but most of the heat stays inside our atmosphere. This process helps to maintain global temperatures within certain limits. It's called a "greenhouse effect" because warmth is sealed inside, just like in a greenhouse.

We've always had greenhouse gases in our atmosphere, and we've always had a natural greenhouse effect on this planet. But what has happened in the past century or so is that human activities have added more greenhouse gases to the atmosphere. As a result, the greenhouse effect has become stronger. With more greenhouse gases in the atmosphere, more energy from Earth is absorbed. This has led to a heating of Earth's surface. In the past 100 years, scientists have found an increase of one degree centigrade in the average temperature on Earth. While there has been some debate, I think people have realized that the increased greenhouse effect is causing the problem of global warming.

Lecture Part 2: "Effects of Global Warming"

Listening for cause and effect, page 115

CD2
TR19 An increase of one degree centigrade in Earth's temperature may not seem like a lot, but it actually causes many changes on our planet. What are the consequences of this increase in Earth's temperature? Today, I'd like to focus on two effects of global warming. The first is an increase in sea level. The sea level has risen over the past 100 years, between about 15 and 25 centimeters. It is rising now and will continue to rise in the future. Some of this rise is due to the heating of the ocean surface. When ocean waters warm, they expand, or get bigger, and so the sea level rises. Another cause is melting ice and snow. The melt water is entering the ocean and resulting in a rise in sea level.

Changes in the weather are another consequence of global warming. As Earth's temperatures continue to rise, some areas of the world will become wetter and some will become drier. Already many countries around the world are experiencing more and longer periods of drought, in other words, long periods of time without enough rain. In fact, the amount of land affected by drought has doubled since the 1970s. Another example of weather change is an increase in severe storm activity. Some scientists believe that if global warming continues, we will have more hurricanes. Hurricanes develop over warm oceans, and so the rise in ocean temperatures may cause more and perhaps stronger hurricanes.

Today I told you about just two effects of global warming: a rise in sea level, and changes in the weather. There are many other consequences of global warming. It's difficult to predict the future. But unless we change the way we do things today — which means we must stop relying on fossil fuels for 80 percent of our energy supply — the amount of greenhouse gases will continue to increase, and temperatures will continue to go up. Scientists predict that this century temperatures will rise to about three degrees centigrade higher than they are now. Sea levels are also likely to go higher, about 60 centimeters above their current level.

So, global warming is a real problem for all of us. It may be the most serious problem in our world today. And I think all of us, as individuals, must take action to solve this problem.

Unit 4: Life on Earth
CD2
TR20 ## Chapter 7: Plants and Animals

Getting Started:
Listening for specific information, page 127

1. The blue whale is the largest animal in the world. Many scientists think that the blue whale is the largest animal that has ever existed on Earth. It can grow up to 33 meters long and weigh as much as 150 tons. Its heart is the same size as a small car. The blue whale's natural habitat is the deepest waters of all the world's oceans.

2. The Venus flytrap is a very unusual plant because it is a plant that eats meat. The Venus flytrap catches insects in its leaves and then eats them! This plant's natural habitat is in the United States, but now it grows all over the world.

3. The platypus is a very unusual animal. It has a bill and webbed feet like a duck, but it has a wide, flat tail. It lives on land but is a very good swimmer. The platypus lives only in Australia.

4. Trees are the biggest plants in the world. The largest type of tree on Earth is the giant sequoia. The natural habitat of the giant sequoia is the mountains of California. These trees can grow to be more than 100 meters tall.

5. Almost half of all insects on Earth are beetles. Scientists have already found 350,000 different kinds of beetles. They can live everywhere, except for the ocean and cold polar regions. The beetle pictured here is the Goliath beetle, the largest and heaviest insect on Earth.

6. Many people think that bamboo is a kind of tree. But, actually, bamboo is a type of grass. Bamboo is the fastest-growing plant on Earth; it can grow four centimeters in just one hour! Bamboo can be found in many different habitats, from cold mountains to hot tropical jungles.

Interview 1: A Green Thumb
CD2
TR21 ### Listening for specific information, page 129

Interviewer: Frank, your hobby is gardening, right? How did you get started?

Frank: Well, let me take you back a long, long time. When I was a kid, everybody had gardens. Wherever we could find a little space, we'd plant some vegetables, like tomatoes, or something like that.

Interview: Did you grow vegetables because you could eat them?

Frank: We didn't have a lot of money back then, so yes, we planted and grew things we could eat. And so because I grew up in that situation, I was always interested in planting and growing things. These days, I enjoy growing native plants.

Interviewer: What does that mean, native plants?

Frank: Native plants are plants that are originally from the area in which they are found. So I like to look for and collect plants that grow in my neighborhood.

Interviewer: What got you interested in native plants?

Frank: Well, one of the reasons is, to collect native plants I have to go to places where other people don't go. I don't like to go where lots of other people have already been. I like to get off the trail.

Interviewer: So you like the challenge of finding and collecting the plants?

Frank: Yes. And there's something else I like, too. I like to share with other people who are also interested in native plants.

Interviewer: Vickie, how about you? What attracted you to gardening?

Vickie: Well, when I was young, everyone was trying to be more green and natural and grow their own food. I tried it too and found out I was good at growing plants. I just kind of had a knack for it.

Interviewer: What sort of plants were you growing?

Vickie: When I started, I only had a small apartment, so I was growing houseplants. I also had a few tomato plants and some herbs.

Interviewer: OK.

Vickie: And then, when I bought a house, I started to do more gardening outside. Now what I do is mostly perennials. That's really my love now, the perennials.

Interviewer: Can you explain what a perennial is?

Vickie: Well, basically, there are two kinds of plants, annuals and perennials. Perennials are plants that come back year after year.

Interviewer: Oh, that makes sense! Because "perennial" means "for a long time."

Vickie: Annuals are the ones that die in the winter, and they don't come back. Perennials look like they die in the fall, but they've really just become inactive. They come back up again in the spring, and that's what I find so exciting. Most perennials go through that cycle for years and years. Some plants even live longer than humans! You plant them and your grandchildren will have the same plants. I really like that.

Interviewer: You said that you have a knack for growing plants. Why is that? What makes your plants grow better?

Vickie: You know the expression "having a green thumb"? I guess that's what I have. But I think it's just an ability to notice little differences.

Interviewer: Differences in the plants?

Vickie: The plants, and their environment. You see a plant that's doing well in an environment, so you try to continue the same kind of care. If you have a plant that's not doing well, you have to find out, is there too much sun? Is there not enough sun? Is there enough water? Is there too much water?

Interviewer: I see. Vickie, is it true that gardening makes people feel calm and relaxed?

Vickie: Well, it's true for me. I go out to my garden and I get right down, put my hands into the dirt, smell the plants, and I can forget about my day-to-day troubles. When I'm in the garden, I don't think about my worries and responsibilities. I feel very connected to the earth, very relaxed and focused. And . . . so for me, it's very calming.

🔊 Interview 2: The Galapagos Islands

CD2 TR22 **Listening for examples,** page 131

Interviewer: Reggie, you went to the Galapagos Islands. Why did you go, and how long did you stay?

Reggie: Well, I was there for about five weeks. I decided to volunteer there because I'd heard so much about it . . . you know, we all dream about going to the Galapagos.

Interviewer: What is it about the Galapagos Islands that's so special?

Reggie: The number one reason why people really want to go to the Galapagos is the diversity of the wildlife. There are so many different and unique animals there, it really is special.

Interviewer: And did you get to see some of the diverse wildlife?

Reggie: Absolutely. You don't have to go far before you see wildlife. For example, on the day I arrived, I was traveling from the airport and I saw Galapagos sea lions right away. I'd been there only 20 minutes and I saw sea lions. They were sleeping on benches meant for people!

Interviewer: Can you give me some other examples of animals you saw there?

Reggie: Well, I saw a lot of birds. Many different kinds of birds, like blue-footed boobies, red-footed boobies, albatross . . . also pelicans, flamingos, and penguins. Those are some of the birds I remember.

Interviewer: That sounds amazing!

Reggie: Yeah. But here's what surprised me. There's been a lot of environmental damage already, so the idea that it's an untouched environment is wrong. Let me give you an example: There used to be 13 subspecies of Galapagos giant tortoises, but now two are extinct. And a third subspecies of tortoise is almost extinct.

Interviewer: OK, some people might ask, "Is there really a problem if a few subspecies of tortoises disappear? We still have 10 others." What would you say to those people?

Reggie: Well, I'd say that it shows a lack of understanding . . . because any ecosystem is so closely connected that even one small thing can change the balance and destroy the system. For instance, there's a tree that one kind of bird uses for food and shelter. If you cut down the tree, you lose the bird, too.

Interviewer: So losing even one plant or one animal can have a bad effect.

Reggie: That's right. And if we lose a living thing, we can't get it back. Once it's gone, it's gone.

 Lecture: John Norris, "What is a Living Thing?"

Before the Lecture: Listening for expressions of contrast, page 136

CD2 TR23

1. Plants, for example, grow taller and wider throughout their lives. Animals start growing as soon as they are born. Unlike plants, however, they usually stop growing when they become adults.

2. I'm sure you can think of many examples of different kinds of animal movement: walking, flying, swimming . . . Plants move, too, but not in the same way as animals.

3. Plants have a very special way of getting food — they make it themselves. To make their own food, plants take a gas called carbon dioxide out of the air. They combine the carbon dioxide with water and sunlight to make food. This food is stored inside the plant and used when the plant needs energy. Animals, on the other hand, cannot make their own food.

4. The process of respiration helps to change the food into energy. Now, animals take in oxygen by breathing in air, whereas plants take in oxygen through tiny holes in their leaves.

5. During reproduction, plants and animals make more of their own kind. Animals have babies or lay eggs. In contrast, most plants make seeds, which fall onto the soil and grow into new plants.

 Lecture Part 1: "Growth, Movement, and Sensitivity"

Checking your notes, page 139

CD2 TR24

Welcome to today's biology lecture, everyone. Biology is the study of all living things on our planet. But, what do we mean when we say "living thing"? What does it mean to be alive? Well, scientists have a very clear way to answer that question. When scientists want to check if something is living or nonliving, they look for seven life processes, or seven special actions that all living things must do. The seven life processes are movement, reproduction, sensitivity, growth, nutrition, respiration, and excretion. These seven actions are like a checklist. If something has all seven, it's a living thing. But even if one process is missing, then it cannot be called a living thing. As you can see, this checklist is very important to biologists, so in our lecture today, let's look at each life process in more detail.

I'll start with two life processes that are easy to observe and understand: growth and movement. All living things grow, which means they increase in size. Plants, for example, grow taller and wider throughout their lives. Animals start growing as soon as they are born. Unlike plants, however, they usually stop growing when they become adults. All

living things also move. I'm sure you can think of many examples of different kinds of animal movement: walking, flying, swimming . . . Plants move, too, but not in the same way as animals. Plants move their roots down into the earth and their leaves up towards the sky. Some flowers open in the morning and close at night. Of course, the movement of a plant is much slower than the movement of an animal. An interesting similarity between plants and animals is that they all move for the same reasons: to get food, to find a safe place to live, and to escape from danger.

Let's move on to the third life process on our checklist. This next process is called sensitivity. What that means is that living things notice their environment and respond to changes in their environment. Animals take in information about their environment by using their senses; in other words, they see, hear, smell, taste, and feel things around them. Plants also take in information about their environment. Although plants do not have as many senses as animals, they do notice changes in water and light. The sunflower got its name because it turns its flower to follow the sun all day long.

 Lecture Part 2: "Nutrition, Respiration, Excretion, and Reproduction"

Organizing your notes in a chart, page 140

CD2 TR25

The next two processes are nutrition and respiration. You've probably heard of nutrition before — that's the process of getting food, and all living things need food for energy. Plants have a very special way of getting food — they make it themselves. To make their own food, plants take a gas called carbon dioxide out of the air. They combine the carbon dioxide with water and sunlight to make food. This food is stored inside the plant and used when the plant needs energy. Animals, on the other hand, cannot make their own food. Because of this, they have to eat plants, or eat other animals that have eaten plants.

OK, so once food is inside a plant or animal, the next life process begins: respiration. And what is respiration? The process of respiration helps to change the food into energy. Now, animals take in oxygen by breathing in air, whereas plants take in oxygen through tiny holes in their leaves. In other words, we see that both plants and animals need and use oxygen to change food into energy inside their bodies. All living things need energy to support all the other life processes, so you can see why nutrition and respiration are so important.

During respiration and the other life actions, plants and animals create waste materials. These are extra materials that a living thing doesn't need, or want. If the waste isn't removed, it will become harmful. Plants pass waste through their leaves and through their roots. Animals move waste out of their bodies in their breath, sweat, urine, and excrement.

To quickly review, then, all living things grow, move, react, eat, respire, and excrete. All living things also grow old and finally die, so the final life process — reproduction — is necessary for life to continue into the future. During reproduction, plants and animals make more of their own kind. Animals have babies or lay eggs. In contrast, most plants make seeds, which fall onto the soil and grow into new plants.

All right, that's our checklist! For something to be called "living" it must show all seven life processes: movement, growth, sensitivity, nutrition, respiration, excretion, and reproduction. Usually we can easily identify something as living, but remember, it must meet all seven life processes. An automobile moves, an automobile can be sensitive, an automobile requires nutrition like gas, and it excretes smoke. But, is it alive?

Unit 4: Life on Earth
CD2 TR26 **Chapter 8: Humans**

Getting Started:

Listening to directions, page 143

Task One.

Look at the picture in your book. Put the palm of your right hand down on top of a desk or table. Keep your arm relaxed. Put your left hand on the upper part of your right arm. Now press gently down on the table with your right palm. Use your left hand to feel the muscles in your upper arm.

Now place your right palm under the desk or table. Push your hand gently up against the table. Use your left hand to feel the muscles in your upper arm.

Now answer the question in your book.

Task Two.

Place your hands on your sides, just above your waist, so that you can feel your ribs. Notice how your ribs move out when you breathe in, then fall back down when you breathe out. When you hear the beep, count the number of breaths you take in 10 seconds. One "in" plus one "out" equals one breath. Try to breathe naturally, without changing or controlling your breathing rate. Are you ready? OK, start! [beep] [beep] Stop. Write the number of breaths you took in your book. Multiply that number by six. This is your average breathing rate per minute.

Task Three.

Find the pulse on the inside of your wrist. Place your first two fingers on your pulse point, as shown in the picture. Try to relax and let your fingers rest lightly on your wrist. When you hear the beep, count the number of beats you feel in 10 seconds. Are you ready? OK, start! [beep] [beep] Stop. Write the number of beats you counted in your book. Multiply that number by six. This is your average heartbeat rate.

Interview 1: Running Track
CD2 TR27 **Listening for main ideas, page 147**

Interviewer: Becca, you were an athlete when you were a student, is that right?

Becca: Yes. I was on the track and field team in college.

Interviewer: What kinds of training did you do?

Becca: The training, well, the coaches really break it down into steps. So, the first step was a lot of weight lifting, like good, strong weight lifting. Then, the next step was cardiovascular training. . .

Interviewer: Did you say *cardiovascular* training? What does that mean, exactly — training to help you breathe better?

Becca: Breathe better, yes, but also to make your heart stronger and to make your whole cardiovascular system work more efficiently.

Interviewer: And what kinds of exercises did you do for cardiovascular training?

Becca: Well, first, we would get a good warm-up, you know, with a three- to five-mile run. After that, we did drills. With drills, you practice running form; that is, the best positions for your body when running. You practice the drills over and over again until your body remembers the positions.

Interviewer: Long runs, drills … anything else?

Becca: Next came the track workouts.

Interviewer: And that's running around a track?

Becca: Yes. These are shorter distances, but faster and with breaks in between. The coach would have us run really hard for a minute, then take a break for five minutes, until we were fully rested, and then go right back into sprinting for another minute.

Interviewer: Can you explain how all of these different exercises helped your body?

Becca: Well, the long-distance running, that's really good for cardiovascular training, because you're running at a slower pace but for a long time, so you build up your lungs and heart. And sprinting — the fast, short running — is good for strengthening your muscles.

Interviewer: So really the muscles and the cardiovascular system are closely related.

Becca: Very closely, especially because, when you're running, your muscles need oxygen so that they can work. When you run, you start breathing faster and harder, right? That's because your muscles need more oxygen. So you breathe in more air and the oxygen goes into your lungs, your blood, and your muscles. So the cardiovascular system and the muscular system are very closely connected.

Interviewer: It sounds like running is a really good sport to make your body stronger and healthier.

Becca: Definitely!

Interview 2: Eat to Live, Don't Live to Eat

CD2 TR28 ### Listening for specific information, page 149

Interviewer: Louise, you're a registered dietician. Why is good nutrition so important?

Louise: You need to eat to live, basically.

Interviewer: It's the basic idea, but people don't think about that.

Louise: Because I think more people, instead of eating to live, they live to eat. In our society, so many activities are centered around food. You have a special event, and you go out for dinner. It's a holiday, so you buy some candy. A lot of our social events are centered around food, and I think that's part of the problem.

Interviewer: What's a healthier way to think about food? How can people remember that we need to eat to live?

Louise: Just think of what your body really needs. There are some basic food groups that people should eat every day, such as grains, vegetables, fruits, and certain kinds of fats.

Interviewer: We should eat fat every day?

Louise: *Good* fats. Also, fiber, and vitamins and minerals. Those six nutrients are your body's basic needs.

Interviewer: So as long as we eat all of those things every day, we'll have a healthy diet?

Louise: Right. And of course, you have to be careful of how much you eat. You don't want to eat too much of any one thing.

Interviewer: Can you explain how these different food groups help the human body?

Louise: Yes, absolutely. Let's start with fiber. I talk to my patients about fiber, because fiber can help lower your cholesterol. If you have fiber in your diet and you also have some cholesterol in your body, the fiber can actually pull the cholesterol out of your blood.

Interviewer: So that's good?

Louise: Yes, it's good. I should point out that cholesterol is a natural part of our cells — you can't get rid of cholesterol. But there's "good" cholesterol, which isn't a problem, and "bad" cholesterol." "Bad" cholesterol is what clogs our blood vessels.

Interviewer: Now, how about protein?

Louise: Yes, you need protein. Protein has a lot of different functions, but mostly you need protein for your body to grow, and to build muscles. That's the main role, to build and repair our muscles.

Interviewer: Protein for strong muscles. Got it. And carbohydrates and fats?

Louise: Those are your energy sources. We need a lot of energy every day, so that's why carbs are so important. And I know people think fats are bad, but you need fats to help protect your organs and to provide energy, too.

Interviewer: Are there foods you can eat to build strong bones?

Louise: For bones, you should look at calcium and vitamin D. Those go hand in hand. You always hear about calcium because that's basically what makes your bones. But you need vitamin D to absorb the calcium from food.

Interviewer: It sounds like you can't eat only one kind of food. You need to have a mix of many different kinds of food.

Louise: Exactly. And to be healthy, you have to have good eating habits, and also exercise. I cannot stress that enough.

Interviewer: Louise, I feel like there is so much need for this type of information right now. I'm just thinking of all of the problems that Americans are having with diet and nutrition.

Louise: Mm-hm. I really enjoy helping people with the little things that can help them in their everyday life: Eat breakfast. Drink water. Cut back on coffee. Small, easy steps that people can see making a difference. That's empowering.

Lecture: Anthony Modesto, "Systems of the Human Body"

CD2 TR29 ### Before the Lecture: Listening for expressions of time order, page 153

1. This phase can last for several hours, and when it's over, the food has become a thick soup.
2. From the stomach, it then moves into the small intestine, where something very important happens.
3. After taking all of the nutrients out of the food, the body doesn't need the leftover food anymore.
4. When we breathe, air enters our body through our mouth and nose. Next, it travels through an airway into our lungs.
5. Finally, the blood returns to the heart, ready to begin the cycle all over again.

Lecture Part 1: "The Digestive System"

CD2 TR30 ### Taking notes in a flowchart, page 155

Have you ever thought about all the things that happen inside your body? The human body, like all living organisms, has many different systems, which is the topic of our lecture today. A body system is defined as a group of organs that work together to carry out a very specific function. Humans have 11 different body systems. These systems carry out every function necessary for life. When your body is healthy, the systems work together very smoothly. But if even one of the systems breaks down, you'd be in big trouble. You wouldn't be able to survive.

Today, I'd like to focus on three of the 11 human body systems: the digestive system, the cardiovascular system, and the respiratory system. These three systems each have their own role in the body, but they also work together in very important ways. Together, they bring oxygen and nutrients to every part of the body. Of course, humans need oxygen and nutrients to live, so our digestive, cardiovascular, and respiratory systems are really important.

OK, where should I start? We all like to eat, so maybe I'll start with the digestive system. Our bodies use the energy in the food we eat to carry out all of our daily life functions. To get the energy from food, our body has to break it down and take the nutrients out of it. This process is called digestion. Digestion begins as soon as you put food into your mouth. As your mouth moves and chews the food, it becomes softer and breaks apart into smaller pieces. When the pieces of food are small and soft enough to swallow, they travel from your mouth down to your stomach. There in the stomach, powerful muscles squeeze the food and mix it together with chemicals. This phase can last for several hours, and when it's over, the food has become a thick soup. From the stomach, it then moves into the small intestine, where something very important happens. Nutrients from the food pass through the intestine and move into the blood. Those nutrients have now become part of the cardiovascular system, which I'll talk about next.

We're not quite done with digestion — there's one more step. After taking all of the nutrients out of the food, the body doesn't need the leftover food anymore. This waste moves into the large intestine and finally, out of the body. The whole process of digestion, from mouth to large intestine, takes about 24 hours to complete.

Lecture Part 2: "The Respiratory and Cardiovascular Systems"

CD2
TR31 **Taking notes in a flowchart,** page 157

Another important system is the respiratory system. Now, the job of this system is to bring oxygen from the air into the body. When we breathe, air enters our body through our mouth and nose. Next, it travels through an airway into our lungs. The air that enters our lungs is rich with oxygen. Inside the lungs, all of this oxygen passes into our blood. Like food, oxygen is necessary for life. Our body uses oxygen to carry out all of its life functions. We need to breathe about eight liters of air every minute to stay alive, and even more when we exercise. Without oxygen, we would die in just a few minutes.

By now, you've probably figured out that blood has many important roles in the human body. It brings nutrients from food, and oxygen from the air, to every part of our body. Blood is part of the cardiovascular system, and that's what I want to talk about next. The cardiovascular system is made up of three things: our blood, our blood vessels, and the heart. The heart is the source of power in the cardiovascular system. With every beat, the heart pushes blood in a cycle around the body — from the heart to the body, around the body, and finally back to the heart again.

When blood first leaves the heart, it's oxygenated, which just means that it's carrying a lot of oxygen. Vessels carry this oxygenated blood all over the body. One of the places the blood goes to is our small intestine. Do you remember what I said, what happens in the small intestine? That's where the blood picks up nutrients from food. As blood travels around the body, it gives oxygen and nutrients to each cell. When the oxygen in our blood has been used up, blood vessels carry it back to the heart. Then, it's pumped into the lungs to get fresh oxygen from the respiratory system. Finally, the blood returns to the heart, ready to begin the cycle all over again. The entire cycle — from heart to body and back to heart, to lungs and back to heart again — takes only 20 seconds.

Well, that's a pretty simple overview, but I hope you can see how these three systems — digestive, respiratory, and cardiovascular — work together to maintain life. The digestive system brings nutrients into the body. The respiratory system brings oxygen into the body. The cardiovascular system carries nutrients and oxygen to the cells. Today, we talked about only three of the body's 11 systems. When you consider that there are eight other equally important systems, you can see that the human body is truly amazing.